Sri Lankan Cookbook

Traditional Sri Lankan Recipes Made Easy

Copyright 2018 by Grizzly Publishing - All rights reserved.

This document is geared towards providing exact and reliable information in regards to the topic and issue covered. The publication is sold with the idea that the publisher is not required to render an accounting, officially permitted, or otherwise, qualified services. If advice is necessary, legal or professional, a practiced individual in the profession should be ordered.

- From a Declaration of Principles which was accepted and approved equally by a Committee of the American Bar Association and a Committee of Publishers and Associations.

In no way is it legal to reproduce, duplicate, or transmit any part of this document in either electronic means or in printed format. Recording of this publication is strictly prohibited and any storage of this document is not allowed unless with written permission from the publisher. All rights reserved.

The information provided herein is stated to be truthful and consistent, in that any liability, in terms of inattention or otherwise, by any usage or abuse of any policies, processes, or directions contained within is the solitary and utter responsibility of the recipient reader. Under no circumstances will any legal responsibility or blame be held against the publisher for any reparation, damages, or monetary loss due to the information herein, either directly or indirectly.

Respective authors own all copyrights not held by the publisher.

The information herein is offered for informational purposes solely and is universal as so. The presentation of the information is without a contract or any type of guarantee assurance.

The trademarks that are used are without any consent, and the publication of the trademark is without permission or backing by the trademark owner. All trademarks and brands within this book are for clarifying purposes only and are the owned by the owners themselves, not affiliated with this document.

www.grizzlypublishing.com

Table of Contents

INTRODUCTION 1

CHAPTER ONE: SRI LANKAN BREAKFAST RECIPES 3

- SAKKARAI PONGAL (SWEET PONGAL) 3
- ROASTED PLAIN FLOUR PUTTU 5
- TAPIOCA WITH FRESH COCONUT 6
- LAVARIYA (SWEET DUMPLING STRING HOPPERS) 7
- CHICKEN FRIED RICE 9
- SINNAKKU KIRIBATH (CUP MILK RICE) 11
- HOPPERS (APPA) 13
- BANANA BREAD 15
- SWEET CLASSIC PANI POL (COCONUT PANCAKES) 16
- TARKA DHAL 20
- SUMMER VEG LASAGNE 22
- KEDGEREE 24

CHAPTER TWO: SRI LANKAN LUNCH RECIPES 26

- SRI LANKAN STYLE CHICKEN CURRY 26
- CHICKPEA CURRY 28
- SPICY CHICKEN NIBBLES 30
- ROASTED COCONUT FISH CURRY 32
- VEGETABLE KURMA 35
- CREAMY CARROT CURRY 37
- SRI LANKAN BRINJAL SAMBOL 39
- CHICKEN XACUTI WITH CHILI SAUCE 40
- FRIED VERMICELLI NOODLES 43
- TANDOORI CHICKEN 45
- MUTTON PEPPER FRY 47
- SPICY CHICKEN MASALA 49
- AMMA'S CHICKEN BIRYANI 51
- SOYA MEAT CURRY 53
- SRI LANKAN SOUR FISH CURRY (AMBUL THIYAL) 55
- POT ROAST YOGURT CHICKEN 57
- SRI LANKAN DATE CHUTNEY 59
- GRILLED SPICY SQUIDS 60
- CLAYPOT DARK CHICKEN AND EGG RICE 62

CHAPTER THREE: SRI LANKAN DINNER RECIPES 64

- Crab Curry with Roasted Coconut 64
- Dal Methi 66
- Aloo Gobi 67
- Peter Kuruvita's Beetroot Curry 69
- Sri Lankan Style Vegetable Fried Rice 70
- Seer Fish in Vinegar and Mustard Sauce 72
- Sri Lankan Pork Badun Curry (Deviled Pork) 74
- Sri Lankan Sates 76
- Sri Lankan Coconut Dhal with Crispy Onions 78
- Sri Lankan Shrimp Curry 80
- Sri Lankan Meatball Curry 82
- Sri Lankan Black Pepper Chicken Curry. 84
- Sri Lankan Rice and Chicken Congee (Kanji) 86
- Sri Lankan Beef Smore 89
- Sri Lankan Vegetable Curry 91

CHAPTER FOUR: SRI LANKAN DESSERT RECIPES 94

- Jaggery Chip Coconut Cookies 94
- Rava Kesari 95
- Corn Flour Muskat/Halwa 97
- 1 Minute Eggless Chocolate Brownie 99
- Sri Lankan Rulang Aluwa 100
- Chocolate Swiss Roll Cake 101
- Ultimate Ginger Toffee 103
- Milk (Maid) Peda 104
- Rava Ladoo (Semolina Laddu) 105
- Condensed Milk Ice Cream 107
- Family Chocolate Cake 108
- Aluwa 110
- Avocado Crazy 112
- Bibikkan (Sri Lankan Coconut Cake) 113
- Sri Lankan Watalappan (Cardamom Spiced Coconut Custard) 114
- Mung Kavum 116
- Love Cake 118
- Sri Lankan Christmas Cake 120

CONCLUSION 122

Introduction

Before we delve into some of the most delicious food on the planet, I first want to thank you for purchasing my book, "Sri Lankan Cookbook: Traditional Sri Lankan Recipes Made Easy." Sri Lanka has long been known for its amazing history, its incredible hospitality, and delightful people. As a result, it has recently become a must see travel destination for those who like to go off the beaten track and experience the depth of untouched and unblemished cultures.

With this increase in popularity has come with the recent exposure of Sri Lankan cuisine to the rest of the western world – in which it has been described to provide some of the best food on the entire planet.

Sri Lankan cuisine is quite unique in that it has been shaped by a combination of historical, cultural, and environmental factors. Historically Sri Lanka has been known as a bit of a trade hub. As a result, regular contact with foreign traders frequently introduced new ingredients and cultural influences into this great country. These influences, when combined with the local traditions of the country's ethnic groups, truly helped build Sri Lankan cuisine into what it has become today.

Some of the staples of modern-day Sri Lankan cuisine include an abundance of rice, decadent coconut, and an absolutely incredibly array of spices – the latter of which is of great respect to the countries local people, being that they have long been considered to be f the best spice traders in the world.

This combination of culture and history offers a point of difference in Sri Lankan food that is not seen in many other countries, as it has created a unique array of amazing flavors and textures that cannot be found anywhere else in the world.

And by integrating meat, poultry, seafood, with the staples of this country, you can quickly imagine why! So, if you are looking for a cookbook that features a wide array of recipes that showcases different flavors, textures and ingredients, then I can guarantee that you have found it.

The recipes in this book include tasty appetizers, entrees, and desserts, all of which have become an integral part of Sri Lankan culture. I can assure you that the recipes mentioned in this book will not only leave you wanting more, but give you a true insight into the intricacies of traditional Sri Lankan cooking. As a bonus, they are easy to understand and even easier to follow. So prepare yourself to take the first step and expand your cooking repertoire, opening your eyes to the wonderful world of Sri Lankan cooking in the process.

Chapter One: Sri Lankan Breakfast Recipes

Sakkarai Pongal (Sweet Pongal)

Serves: 2-3

Ingredients:

- 20g raisins
- 15pcs. cashew nuts
- 3 ½ water
- 2 tablespoons fresh coconut (grated)
- 2 tablespoons sugar
- 2 tablespoons ghee
- ¾ cup jaggery
- ½ cup raw white rice
- ½ red raw rice
- ¼ split yellow lentils/moong dhal
- 1/8 teaspoon cardamom powder
- salt to taste

Method:

1. Wash the rice and lentils with water.
2. Prepare a pressure cooker, add 3 1/2 cups of water with the salt and cook up to 4-5 whistle
3. Heat the ghee in a pan and roast the cashew nuts until golden brown and then add raisins and fry for about 30 seconds.
4. Finely chop the jaggery and add 1/4 cup water and cook in a medium flame for couple of minutes. Add the cardamom powder and sugar.
5. Strain the mixture in a sieve.

6. Add grated coconut, strained jaggery mixture and roasted cashew nuts and raisins.
7. Mix well and cook the pongal in a medium flame for 5 minutes while stirring the mixture.
8. Serve while hot.

Roasted Plain Flour Puttu

Serves: 3

Ingredients:

- 2 cups plain flour
- 2 stalks pandan leaves
- 1 teaspoon salt
- ½ cup fresh coconut (grated)
- warm water (as needed)

Method:

1. Wash and cut the pandan leaves into about 5cm length. Set it aside.
2. Dry roast the plain flour until little brown and fragrant. Set aside to cool.
3. Place the flour in a large wide bowl. Mix salt with warm water in a jug.
4. Slowly pour the warm water to the flour to form a grainy mixture.
5. Boil 1 liter of water in puttu pot or steamer pot.
6. To cook in puttu mould, lay a piece of pandan leaf, and add 2 tablespoons of grated coconut.
7. Add the flour mixture over the coconut; repeat the layering process untill you reach the top of the mould.
8. Finally, lay another piece of pandan leaf on top.
9. To cook in steamer, layer a cloth (cheese cloth) with pandan leaves, then spread the grated coconut over it.
10. Add the flour mixture on top of the coconut in a single or double layer.
11. Remove sweet alternative, serve with jaggery or sugar, banana and with coconut milk.

Tapioca with Fresh Coconut

Serves: 2

Ingredients:

- 200 g tapioca (boiled & cubed)
- 3 pcs. red dry Chili (chopped)
- 2 tablespoons fresh coconut (grated)
- 1 large onion (slice)
- 1 tablespoon oil
- 1 sprig curry leaves
- ½ teaspoon mustard seeds
- ½ teaspoon urad dhal
- ½ teaspoon turmeric powder

Method:

1. Boiled the tapioca over medium heat with a little salt and turmeric.
2. Once cooled, peel the skin and cut into small cubes.
3. Heat oil in a pan; add mustard seeds and urad dhal.
4. Once mustard starts to splutter, add curry leaves, dry chili and onions.
5. Sauté onions until light brown
6. Add cubed tapioca and stir for about 1 minute.
7. Lastly, add grated coconut and give a good stir until tapioca blend well with coconut and spices.
8. Serve hot with sugar or lunu miris.

Lavariya (Sweet Dumpling String Hoppers)

Serves: 3-4

Ingredients:

- ½ cup jaggery
- 1 tablespoon water
- ½ cup cooked moong dhal
- ¾ grated coconut
- 2 tablespoons sugar
- ¼ teaspoon cardamom powder
- a dash of salt to taste

Method:

1. Prepare a pressure cooker and add the moong dhal with a pinch of salt for up to 3 whistles. And set aside. Prepare the coconut mixture.
2. Use a heavy bottom pan with medium heat and add jaggery with 1 tablespoon of water and melt the jaggery slowly.
3. Once the jaggery fully melted, add the cooked moong dhal.
4. Add the freshly grated coconut and stir slowly.
5. Add the sugar, cardamom powder along with a pinch of salt. Stir continuously.
6. Keep stirring until the mixture is thick and leaves the sides of the pan. Set aside.
7. In the meantime, prepare the string hopper dough.
8. Place the dough in a string hopper mold and press both of the handle to squeeze onto banana leaf or any oiled paper.
9. Place one heaped teaspoon of the coconut mixture in the center of the string hopper and fold the baking paper/banana leaf.
10. Press the edges to seal properly.

11. Slip the folded lavariya on to steamer and steam for 10 to 15 minutes in batches.

Chicken Fried Rice

Serves: 2

Ingredients:

- 150g chicken breast
- 1 cup basmati rice (left over/cooked rice)
- 2 tablespoon butter
- 2 medium-large eggs
- 2 pcs. medium red onions (slice thinly)
- 1 teaspoon freshly ground black pepper
- ½ medium green capsicum (slice thinly)
- ½ tablespoon ginger and garlic paste
- ½ teaspoon sesame oil
- ½ teaspoon light soy sauce
- ¼ cup leeks/spring onion (slice thinly)
- ¼ cup beans (slice thinly)

- a pinch white pepper (ground)

- salt to taste

Method:

1. Wash and cut the chicken breast into thin strips. Mixed the chicken with ½ teaspoon of salt and pepper. Set aside.
2. In a medium frying pan, heat 2 tablespoon of oil and add the chicken and cooked until brown.
3. In the same pan break the eggs, stirring constantly and cook for 1 minute. Set aside.
4. Heat a medium skillet and add the butter and ginger garlic paste sauté for 1 minute. (Do not burn the butter).

5. Add the capsicum and sauté for about 2 minutes.
6. Add the slice beans and carrots, add a dash of salt.
7. Finally add the leeks/spring onion and sauté for 2 minutes.
8. Sprinkle with the black and white pepper and mix with vegetables.
9. Now add the chicken and cooked eggs with light soy sauce and give a good stir.
10. Then, add the cooked rice and thoroughly mix with other ingredients.
11. Lastly, add sesame oil and stir.
12. Serve hot with ketchup.
13. I usually mix both chili and tomato sauce together.

Sinnakku Kiribath (Cup Milk Rice)

Serves: 4

Ingredients:

- 1 lb white short grain rice (ideally Sri Lankan rice called kekulu)
- 3 cups thick coconut milk
- 5 cups water
- salt to taste

Method:

1. Wash the rice and place in a large saucepan and add the water and salt.
2. Bring to a boil without cover, over medium heat.
3. Reduce heat, cover, and simmer on medium / low heat until water is absorbed and rice is tender (about 20 to 25 minutes).
4. Add the coconut milk and stir well until everything is mixed.
5. Simmer on low heat until the rice absorbs all the coconut milk (about 15 minutes).
6. Remove from fire and let it cool for about 5 minutes.
7. Transfer the mixture to a large shallow dish and flatten with the back of a flat spoon, spatula or parchment paper.
8. Draw lines on the top surface in the shape of diamond or square.
9. Let cool and solidify for about 10 minutes before cutting into pieces.
10. Serve with seeni sambol and/or lunu miris.

Note:

- The proportions of coconut milk and water are approximate. The amount of water and coconut milk depends on the type of rice that is used.
- If the surface of the rice dries too quickly, apply a little coconut milk to rehydrate it.
- In some parts of Sri Lanka, kiribath is traditionally prepared with red rice.

Hoppers (Appa)

Serves: 5

Ingredients:

- 200 ml coconut milk
- 8 cups rice flour
- 4 teaspoon yeast
- 4 teaspoon sugar
- 2 teaspoon oil
- 2 cups water

Method:

1. Mix the ingredients for the yeast mixture and leave for 15 minutes until frothy. If the mixture is not frothy at this point, the yeast you used is too old, you will need to use a new batch.
2. Put the rice flour into a large bowl and add the yeast mixture.
3. Next add the 2 cups water. Mix well
4. Cover the bowl with a wet cloth or plastic wrap and leave for about eight hours in a warm place. The batter should rise to double the original size.
5. Finally, add 3/4 of the coconut milk and 2 tablespoons sugar and stir well. If more liquid is needed, add the remaining of the coconut milk little by little. The batter should be thinner than a pancake batter. Add salt to taste.
6. Soak a small piece of cloth in oil in a saucer. When hot, rub the pan thoroughly with the oiled-cloth. Add about 1/4 cup of the batter to the pan and turn the pan in a

circular motion so that the batter sticks to the sides of the pan.
7. Cover and cook for about a minute under low-medium heat. Use a butter knife to loosen the edges of the hopper and serve hot.
8. Katta sambol or sini sambol used as accompaniment in here.

Banana Bread

Serves: 2-3

Ingredients:

- 2 -3 ripe medium-large bananas
- 3 ½ teaspoon baking powder
- 3 teaspoon orange peel (grated)
- 3 tablespoons vegetable oil (like olive, canola, hydrogenated vegetable oil)
- 2 ½ cups white flour (or you can use 1/2 wheat flour & 1/2 white flour)
- 1 teaspoon salt
- 1 medium-large egg (beat the egg)
- 1 cup walnuts (chopped)
- ½ cup white sugar
- ½ cup brown sugar
- 1/3 cup milk (if it still dry, add another 1/3 cup milk)
- margarine or butter to grease the loaf pan

Method:

1. Mix all the ingredients together except the egg, milk and bananas. Mix well with a spatula. Add the mashed banana and then add 1/3 cup milk. If it is dry, add another 1/3 cup milk.
2. Grease the loaf pan and pour. Bake in the oven at 350C for about 45 - 60 minutes. Poke with toothpick and if the toothpick is clean and nothing was clinging at the side and then it is done.
3. Serve while hot.

Sweet Classic Pani Pol (Coconut Pancakes)

Serves: 20-25 stuffed pancakes

Ingredients:

Coconut filling:

- 6.50 oz/1 cup packed muscovado sugar or grated jaggery in weight (please see note)
- 6 cardamom pods or ¼ tsp ground cardamom
- 1 ½ cups of desiccated coconut or 2 cups freshly grated coconut
- ¾ cup of good quality coconut milk (omit if you're using freshly grated coconut)
- ¼ cup of water
- ¼ teaspoon cinnamon
- pinch of salt to taste

Sri Lankan pancakes (crepes):

- 200 g flour
- 4 medium-large eggs
- 2 tablespoons sugar
- 2 cups of milk
- 1 teaspoon vanilla
- ½ cup oil
- ½ tsp salt (heaped)
- ½ teaspoon baking powder
- ¼ teaspoon turmeric or 4 saffron strands prepared as below

Method:

Sweet coconut filling:

1. Prepare a saucepan and add the coconut milk, heat until it's simmering (not boiling). When it starts to simmer, add the desiccated coconut and stir to combine.
2. Remove from the heat and set it aside to allow the coconut to cool down. This also allows the desiccated coconut to completely absorb the milk. Store the coconut in a bowl, cover and set aside until needed.
3. Combine the sugar, salt, water, cardamom and cinnamon in a saucepan and heat over medium heat while stirring occasionally until the sugar has melted completely.
4. Bring the sugar syrup to a boil. Add the coconut to the sugar syrup and mix well.
5. The coconut sugar mix will be runny, with extra moisture. Cook the mix over medium heat, until the sugar syrup is absorbed by the coconut and you have a sticky coconut mix.
6. Let the mix cool down to room temperature, while you make the crepes.

Saffron strands:

1. Grind the saffron strands along with 1/4 teaspoon sugar and 1/4 salt until the saffron strands are completely ground.
2. Steep the ground saffron mix with 3 tablespoons of hot water and leave it to cool down to room temperature.
3. Add this instead of turmeric, if you prefer.

Sri Lankan pancakes (crepes):

1. **Using a blender** - Place all the ingredients in a blender. Start with the liquid ingredients, and then add the dry ingredients.

2. Blend until you have a smooth crepe batter. Let the crepe batter sit at room temperature, covered, for about 15-30 minutes to rest.
3. **Without a blender** - Place all the dry ingredients in a large bowl. Whisk all the wet ingredients together in a jug.
4. Make a well in the middle of the dry ingredients and slowly pour the wet ingredient mix, while whisking. After adding half of the liquid, whisk the mix to ensure there are no lumps. Add the rest of the liquid and whisk until smooth. Let it rest, covered, for 15 - 30 minutes until you are ready to use it.
5. **Making the crepes** - Heat a 6-inch non-stick pan over medium high heat. Brush some oil on the surface of the pan when it's hot.
6. Pour ¼ cup of the batter to the hot pan, while swirling, to evenly coat the surface of the pan. The batter will create bubbles on the surface if it's hot enough (this is characteristic of Sri Lankan crepes, but it's optional). Cover any big holes with some loose batter.
7. Cook for about 30 seconds, until the edges turn a golden brown.
8. Loosen the crepe and flip it over, and cook it for a further 15 - 30 seconds.
9. Both sides should be a golden to dark golden brown in color.
10. Flip the crepes on to a plate and stack them on top of each other until you have cooked all the crepes.
11. Once all the crepes are cooked, cover the stack with a clean cloth or plastic wrap and let it cool.
12. **A note about the crepes** - If the pan is not as hot, the crepes will take a little longer to cook, and the surface will be smooth (no bubbles), but still flip the crepe when the

edges start to brown. These will then look more like French crepes.

Assembly:

1. Spread about 2 tablespoons of the coconut filling in the center of each crepe. Fold over one end, over the filling. Fold the edges in and roll up the crepe roll to form a log/roll - Similar to how Spring rolls are rolled up.
2. Place the crepes on a plate, with the seam side down.
3. Cover the crepes with a cloth or plastic wrap until needed.
4. Eat them plain, or with a cup of tea. Enjoy!

Note:

- If you are unable to find both - you can use dark brown sugar instead.

Tarka Dhal

Serves: 2

Ingredients:

- 400g red lentils
- 2-3 cloves garlic (finely sliced)
- 2 tablespoons turmeric
- 2 knobs unsalted butter
- 2 teaspoons cumin seeds
- 1-2 fresh green chili, finely sliced (remove seeds if you want to keep the heat down)
- 1 small onion (finely chopped)

Optional (recommended) extras:

- 2-3 medium-large tomatoes (chopped small)
- 1 teaspoon garam masala
- 1 teaspoon ground coriander
- thumb-sized piece of fresh ginger (finely grated)

Method:

1. Place the lentils in a pan and cover with enough cold water to come to around two inches above their surface. Bring to the boil (skin off any scum that rises to the top), and reduce to a simmer. Stir in the turmeric and a generous knob of butter. Cover and leave to cook gently.
2. In a small frying pan, dry-fry the cumin seeds over a medium heat until toasted and fragrant (no more than a couple of minutes). Remove from the pan and set to one side.
3. Melt a second knob of butter in the same frying pan and gently fry the chopped garlic, onion, chilies and the

grated ginger and tomatoes, if you're using them. Once the garlic is golden, mix in the toasted cumin seeds and, if using, the garam masala and ground coriander. Remove from the heat until the lentils are completely softened.

4. Give the lentils a good stir. They should have the consistency of porridge – thicker than soup and looser than humus. Add more water as necessary (you will be surprised how thick they can get over just a couple of extra minutes cooking), and mix in your aromatic fried mixture.

5. Season to taste, then serve on its own, topped with coriander, or with a side of basmati rice and greens.

Summer Veg Lasagne

Serves: 6-8

Ingredients:

- 700g asparagus
- 500g frozen peas
- 500g fresh lasagne sheets
- 300g frozen broad beans
- 300ml single cream
- 300ml organic vegetable stock
- 2 x 250g tubs of cottage cheese
- 1 (60g) big bunch of fresh mint
- ½ x 30g tin of anchovies in oil (from sustainable sources)
- 6 cloves of garlic
- 1 bunch of spring onions
- 1 lemon
- parmesan cheese
- olive oil
- a few sprigs of fresh thyme

Method:

1. Preheat the grill to the maximum setting.
2. Trim and finely slice the spring onions.
3. Pour the oil from the anchovy tin into a large frying pan over a medium-high heat, then add the spring onions and anchovies (save the rest for another day).
4. Using a garlic crusher, crush the garlic straight into the pan and toss everything together well.

5. Line up the asparagus, trim off the woody ends, then finely slice and add the stems to the pan, reserving the tips for later.
6. Season with sea salt and black pepper; add 1 splash of boiling water and cook for a few minutes, or until softened, stirring occasionally.
7. Add the peas and broad beans to the pan, then pick, roughly chop and add the mint along with the cream. Finely grate in half the lemon zest.
8. Roughly mash and squash everything in the pan using a fork or a potato masher, then season to perfection with salt and pepper.
9. Pour in the stock and bring to the boil, then stir in 1 tub of cottage cheese – the consistency should be creamy and loose.
10. Place a deep 30cm x 35cm roasting tray on a medium heat. Spoon in a quarter of the veggie mixture to cover the bottom of the tray, and then top with a layer of lasagne sheets, and a good grating of Parmesan. Repeat the layers with the rest of the veg and pasta, finishing with a layer of lasagne sheets.
11. Mix the remaining tub of cottage cheese with 1 splash of water to loosen, and then spread evenly over the top of the lasagne.
12. Toss the reserved asparagus tips in a drizzle of oil, then tip onto the lasagne, pushing everything down with the back of a spoon to compact.
13. Strip over the thyme leaves and finish with a drizzle of oil and a generous grating of parmesan.
14. Turn the heat under the tray up to high and cook until the lasagne starts to bubble, then place under the grill on the middle shelf for about 8 minutes, or until golden and gorgeous.
15. Served with a seasonal green salad.

Kedgeree

Serves: 6

Ingredients:

- 450g undyed smoked haddock fillets (from sustainable sources)
- 300g brown rice
- 200g leftover cooked greens, such as brussels sprouts, brussels tops, kale, cabbage, broccoli
- 200g frozen peas
- 25g unsalted butter
- 6 medium-large free-range eggs
- 5 cm piece of ginger
- 2 red onions
- 2 cloves of garlic
- 1 fresh red chili
- 1 heaped teaspoon fennel seeds
- 1 heaped teaspoon curry powder
- 1 lemon
- ½ bunch (15g) of fresh coriander
- olive oil

Method:

1. Cook the rice in a pan of boiling salted water according to the packet instructions, then drain and refresh under cold water, leaving it in the colander.
2. At the same time, poach the fish in a large pan of simmering salted water on a medium heat for 10 minutes, and then carefully remove with a slotted spoon. Turn the heat up under the poaching water and bring back to a good simmer.

3. Meanwhile, peel the onions and finely slice with the red chili (de-seed if you like) and coriander stalks. Peel and finely chop the garlic and ginger. Place it all in a large frying pan on a medium heat with 1 tablespoon of oil and the butter, and cook for 10 minutes or until soft but not coloured, stirring occasionally.
4. Crush the fennel seeds in a pestle and mortar, and stir into the pan with the curry powder.
5. Slice and add the leftover greens, along with the frozen peas, then gently fold in the rice with two spoons so it stays nice and fluffy.
6. Flake in the poached fish, gently fold again, season to perfection with sea salt, black pepper and lemon juice, and then keep on a low heat for just 3 or 4 minutes while you poach the eggs to your liking in the simmering water.
7. Place the eggs on top of the kedgeree, scatter over the coriander leaves, and a little extra chili, if you fancy, and then tuck in. Delicious served with mango chutney, or dollops of lemon-spiked yoghurt.

Tips:

- Add a squeeze of lemon juice and a handful of coriander to infuse the poaching water for an extra hit of flavor – delicious!

Chapter Two: Sri Lankan Lunch Recipes

Sri Lankan Style Chicken Curry

Serves: 4

Ingredients:

- 4 medium chicken thighs
- 2-3 cardamom seeds
- 2 cups coconut milk
- 2 garlic cloves (chopped)
- 2 green chilies (sliced)
- 2 tablespoons coconut oil
- 2 cloves
- 2 tablespoons tamarind juice
- 2 tablespoons roasted curry powder
- 1 tablespoon chili powder
- 1 knorr chicken cube
- 1 cinnamon stick
- ½ teaspoon turmeric
- ½ an onion (sliced)
- curry leaves & rampe
- salt and pepper to taste

Method:

1. Heat coconut oil in a medium saucepan and add garlic, onion, green chili, cardamom, cloves, cinnamon stick, rampe and curry leaves. Sauté for a few minutes.
2. Add chicken thighs, knorr chicken cube, turmeric, roasted curry powder, chili powder, tamarind juice and

coconut milk into the saucepan. Cook until the chicken is done and the gravy is thick.
3. Add salt and pepper for seasoning and pour curry into a serving bowl.
4. Garnish with tomato wedges or thinly sliced green chilies on top (optional) and serve hot.

Chickpea Curry

Serves: 2

Ingredients:

- 250g chickpeas/kadala (soak overnight for 7-8 hours)
- 3 green Chilies
- 2 medium-large red onions (sliced)
- 2 tablespoons thick coconut milk
- 2 medium-large tomatoes
- 1 tablespoon Ginger garlic paste
- 1 spring curry leaves
- 1 tablespoon coriander leaves (chopped)

To temper:

- 3 cloves
- 3 whole cardamom
- 1 teaspoon cumin seeds
- 1 bay leaf
- ½ tablespoon cooking oil
- 1/8-inch cinnamon stick

Spices:

- 1 teaspoon chili powder
- ¼ turmeric powder
- 1 tablespoon coriander powder
- 1 teaspoon garam masala
- salt to taste

Method:

1. Start by soaking the chickpeas/kadala over night for at least 7-8 hours. Pressure cooks the chickpeas with 2 cups of water and ¼ teaspoon of salt (after soaking) up to 4 to 5 whistles or until done. (Cooking time will be approximately 20-25 minutes). Set aside the chickpea water for later use.
2. Grind the tomato into puree. Set aside.
3. Heat oil in a frying pan; add cumin seeds, cinnamon sticks, cardamom, cloves and bay leaf. Sauté for about 30 seconds or until it turns soft.
4. Add sliced onion, curry leaves and sliced green chilies. Sauté for about 1 minute.
5. Add pureed tomato and ginger garlic paste and sauté well.
6. After few minutes, add ground chili powder, coriander powder, turmeric powder and garam masala and then continue sautéing.
7. Add reserved (boiled) chickpea water.
8. Boil the gravy for about 5-6 minutes. If you want more gravy, add ¼ cup water.
9. Now you can add the boiled chickpeas/kadala.
10. Left the curry to cook for another 8-10 minutes. Check the salt and adjust to taste.
11. Finally add the coconut milk and stir well. Cook for another 2 minutes.
12. Garnish with chopped coriander leaves.
13. Serve with rice; chapathi, puttu or with string hoppers.

Spicy Chicken Nibbles

Serves: 2-3

Ingredients:

- 500g chicken nibbles
- 4 tablespoons dry red chili flakes (adjust according to your taste)
- 3 tablespoons chili sauce
- 2 teaspoons ginger paste
- 2 teaspoons garlic paste
- 2 tablespoons rice flour
- 2 tablespoons cooking oil (as needed)
- 1 tablespoon light soy sauce
- 1 tablespoon tomato sauce
- 1 sprig curry leaves
- 1 pandan leaves
- 1 teaspoon sugar
- 1 tablespoon coriander powder
- ½ tablespoon black pepper powder
- ½ teaspoon fennel seeds
- ¼ teaspoon turmeric powder
- ¼ teaspoon cumin powder
- salt to taste

Method:

1. Blend the red dry chilies, black pepper, fennel seeds, coriander powder, turmeric powder, rice flour, cumin powder, sugar, soy sauce, chili sauce, tomato sauce, ginger garlic paste and salt.
2. Rub this mixture thoroughly to the chicken nibbles and marinate for about 30 minutes. Set aside. Heat the oil in

a frying pan (or wok) and add the marinated chicken nibbles with curry leaves and pandan leaves.
3. Cook until the mixture become slightly dry.
4. Check the salt and cook for another 1 minute and garnish with curry leaves.
5. This dry chicken dish will go absolutely delicious with fried rice.

Roasted Coconut Fish Curry

Serves: 2-3

Ingredients:

- 100g fresh coconut (grated)
- 1 ¼ teaspoon cumin seeds
- 1 teaspoon fennel seeds

For Onion mixture:

- 1 medium onion (chopped)
- 5 cloves garlic
- 1 cm ginger

For the curry:

- 750g fish (any kind to your liking)
- 100g medium onion/1 large shallots (sliced)
- 75g tamarind pulp
- 3 tablespoons coriander leaves (chopped)
- 2 medium-large tomatoes
- 2 green chilies
- 1 teaspoon fenugreek seeds
- 1 teaspoon red chili powder
- 1 sprig curry leaves
- 1 pandan/rampe leaf
- 1 cinnamon stick
- 1 tablespoon cooking oil (or as needed)
- ¾ teaspoon coriander powder
- ¼ teaspoon mustard seeds
- ¼ teaspoon cumin Seeds
- ¼ teaspoon turmeric powder

- ¼ teaspoon cumin powder
- salt to taste

Method:

1. Clean, wash and cut the fish into curry pieces.
2. Dry roast the cumin seeds and fennel seeds over low-medium heat.
3. In a same pan, roast the coconut until golden brown and fragrant. Set aside to allow it to cool and blend with roasted cumin and fennel seeds.
4. Use the same pan to sauté the onion, garlic and ginger with 1 teaspoon of oil for about 1 minute. Set aside to cool and grind to a smooth paste.
5. Chop the tomatoes and blend coarsely in a blender. Set aside.
6. Soak the tamarind pulp in 1 cup of water.
7. Heat oil in a pan and fry the mustard seeds, cinnamon stick, cumin seeds and fenugreek and fry over a low heat until aromatic.
8. Add sliced onion, curry leaves, green chilies and rampe/pandan leaves. Sauté until onion is golden brown.
9. Add the ground onion mixture and sauté for about 1-2 minutes.
10. Add the ground tomatoes and sauté for another 1 minute.
11. Add all the masala powders along with the salt and sauté over low heat until oil separates.
12. Add the ground coconut mixture and mix thoroughly with the other ingredients.
13. Strain the soaked tamarind water and add to the sautéed mixture.
14. Add enough water for the gravy and boil for about 5-10 minutes until mixture smells cooked.

15. Gently lower the fish pieces into boiling gravy.
16. Cook over medium heat until fish pieces are cooked for about 10-15 minutes.
17. Garnish with chopped coriander leaves and serve with hot rice.

Vegetable Kurma

Serves: 2-3

Ingredients:

- 150g coconut (grated)
- 20g cashew nuts (soaked)
- 20g green peas
- 3 cloves
- 3 green beans
- 2 cardamom
- 2 medium-large carrots
- 2 medium-large potatoes
- 2 small green chilies
- 2 tablespoons oil
- 1 ¼ teaspoon red chili powder
- 1 teaspoon garam masala powder
- 1 large onion (chopped)
- 1 large tomato (chopped)
- 1 tablespoon ginger garlic paste
- 1 sprig curry leaves
- 1 bay leaf
- 1 cinnamon stick (broken into pieces)
- Half cauliflower
- ¼ teaspoon cumin seeds
- ¼ teaspoon mustard seeds
- ¼ cup coriander leaves (chopped)
- ¼ teaspoon turmeric powder
- ¼ teaspoon coriander powder
- ¼ teaspoon cumin powder
- salt to taste

Method:

1. Soak the cashew nuts in hot water for about 10 minutes.
2. Chop all the vegetable into small cubes/pieces.
3. Grind the coconut and cumin seeds into paste and set aside.
4. Heat the oil in a frying pan (or a wok) and fry the mustard seeds, cumin seeds, bay leaf, cardamom, cloves and broken cinnamon sticks.
5. Let the spices sizzle for about 30 seconds.
6. Add the chopped onion and sauté until brown.
7. Add sliced green chilies and curry leaves cook for 30 seconds and add ginger garlic paste, sauté for about 1 minute.
8. Add the chopped tomatoes and cook until soft.
9. Add all the ground masala powders and stir well.
10. Add the vegetable and cook until the vegetables are mixed thoroughly with the spices for 2 minutes. Pour enough water to cover the vegetable and cover with a lid and cook for 10-15 minutes until vegetables are soft.
11. In the meantime, grind the cashew nuts with some water and make a thick paste.
12. Add the cashew nuts paste and stir well.
13. After 5 minutes add the ground coconut paste and cook for 5 minutes, stirring until semi thick.
14. Garnish with the chopped coriander leaves and serve.

Creamy Carrot Curry

Serves: 2-3

Ingredients:

- 400g medium-large carrots
- 4 cloves garlic (chopped)
- 3 green chilies (sliced)
- 1 medium onion (sliced)
- 1 sprig curry leaves
- 1 pandan leaf
- 1 teaspoon coriander powder
- 1 tablespoon cooking oil
- ½ teaspoon red chili powder
- ¼ cup coconut milk (medium thickness)
- ¼ teaspoon fenugreek seeds
- 1/8 teaspoon mustard seeds
- 1/8 teaspoon cumin seeds
- 1/8 teaspoon cumin powder
- 1/8 teaspoon garam masala powder
- salt to taste

Method:

1. Slice the carrots into semi-circle shape.
2. Slice the onion and slice the green chilies.
3. Heat the oil in a frying pan and add mustard seeds, fenugreek seeds and cumin seeds.
4. Let the spices sizzle for about 30 seconds. Add curry leaves, sliced green chilies and broken pandan leaf pieces and sauté for about 30 seconds.
5. Add chopped garlic and sauté.
6. Now add sliced onion and cook the onions until golden.

7. Add the carrots and sauté until carrots are soft enough.
8. Add all the ground masala powders and salt to taste.
9. Pour some water and sauté for about one minute.
10. Add coconut milk and cook over medium heat for 20 minutes or until thick and creamy.
11. Serve with bread, roti or rice.

Sri Lankan Brinjal Sambol

Serves: 1-2

Ingredients:

- 2 medium-large brinjal (eggplant)
- 6 medium onion (chopped)
- 3 green chilies (cut diagonally)
- 2 teaspoon vinegar
- ½ teaspoon ground mustard
- ¼ teaspoon salt
- 1/8 teaspoon turmeric powder
- cooking oil (for deep frying)

Method:

1. Wash and slice the brinjal in rounds.
2. Rub with the turmeric powder and salt.
3. Leave for 5 mins.
4. Heat the oil in a frying pan (or a wok) and deep fry the brinjals in batches till crisp.
5. Drain in a paper towel to remove excess oil.
6. Add chopped onions, sliced green chilies, vinegar, and ground mustard. Mix well.
7. Now add the fried brinjals and mix well with the onion mixture.
8. Serve immediately.

Chicken Xacuti with Chili Sauce

Serves: 2-3

Ingredients:

- 500g chicken
- 3 tablespoons sugar
- 3 tablespoons vegetable oil (or as needed)
- 2 teaspoon Sri Lankan roasted curry powder
- 1 medium-large tomato (chopped)
- 1 teaspoon chili flakes (crushed)
- 1 medium-large onion (sliced)
- 1 tablespoon coriander leaf (chopped)
- ½ tablespoon ginger garlic paste
- 1/8 cumin seeds
- 1/8 teaspoon fennel seeds
- a pinch chili sauce
- some water (for cooking, if necessary)

For xacuti masala:

- 150ml water
- 50g fresh coconut (grated)
- 1-inch piece ginger
- 8 whole black pepper
- 4 garlic
- 4 dry red chilies
- 3 cardamom
- 3 cloves
- 1 green chili
- 1 clove onion (sliced)
- 1 small stick cinnamon

- 1 tablespoon coriander seeds
- 1 teaspoon cumin seeds

Method:

1. Clean the chicken and cut into curry pieces. Mix the chicken with a little salt and set aside.
2. To make Xacuti masala, dry roast the cardamom, cinnamon, cloves, cumin seeds, coriander seeds, black pepper and dry chilies over low flame.
3. In a same pan, dry roast the grated coconut until golden brown.
4. Add the onions, green chilies, ginger and garlic and sauté without oil on a very low heat. Cook until onions are just cooked.
5. Blend the roasted spices first and then blend the roasted coconut along with onion, green chili and ginger garlic paste.
6. Add 100ml water when you blend the mixture. Blend until smooth. Set aside.
7. Heat the oil in a wide pan and add 1/8 cumin seeds, and fennel seeds.
8. Add the remaining sliced onion and sauté until golden brown.
9. Add ginger garlic paste and sauté.
10. While sautéing, the ginger garlic paste, put the chopped tomatoes and cook till tomatoes are well mashed. Add turmeric powder, crushed red chili powder and a pinch of sugar. Stir until well combined.
11. Add half of the ground masala and stir. It depends on how much the gravy you need. (I have added only ¾ of the mixture.)
12. Cook the mixture for about 3 minutes.

13. Put the chicken and cook till tender. Keep on stirring.
14. Add Roasted curry powder and cook for 5 minutes until the oil starts to separate from the pan.
15. Adjust the salt to taste.
16. When the gravy becomes thick add the chili sauce and cook for further 2 minutes.
17. Stir in the chopped coriander leaves.
18. Serve with vegetable fried rice.

Note:

- While blending the Spice and coconut mixture with water cover your blender with a plastic bag. This will help to avoid the mixture from splashing out.

Fried Vermicelli Noodles

Serves: 2-3

Ingredients:

- 350g rice vermicelli
- 100g boneless chicken breast (sliced thinly)
- 2 medium-large eggs
- 1/4-inch ginger (chopped thinly)
- 5 tablespoons water
- 3 tablespoons vegetable oil
- 3 stalks bok choy (shredded)
- 3 tablespoons light soy sauce
- 2 garlic cloves (crushed)
- 2 tablespoons chili sauce
- 2 tablespoons tomato ketchup
- 1 medium onion (sliced)
- ½ tablespoon Sri Lankan vinegar
- ½ tablespoon crushed chili flakes/powder
- ¼ teaspoon cumin powder
- 1 teaspoon sugar (or to taste)
- ½ teaspoon salt (or to taste)

Method:

1. Soak the rice vermicelli in cold water for about 15 minutes until softened but not soggy.
2. Drain well. Using your kitchen scissors, cut into small pieces, about 3-4 inches lengths.
3. Heat 2 teaspoons of oil in shallow frying pan and scramble the eggs. Set aside.
4. Heat 1 tablespoon oil in a pan (or a wok). Fry chicken until lightly brown. Set aside.

5. Add the onions, ginger and garlic stir fry for about 3 minutes until softened but not browned.
6. Add the chili sauce, ketchup, soy sauce, vinegar, cumin powder, crushed chili flakes, sugar and salt. Stir fry for 30 seconds.
7. Add the water. Cook the sauce mixture for 1-2 minutes.
8. Add cooked chicken, vegetable and stir fry for 2-3 minutes.
9. Add drained rice vermicelli noodles and scrambled eggs. Stir fry vigorously for 2 minutes.
10. Serve immediately.

Notes:

- You can use thinly sliced beef/pork or even cooked prawns.
- You can add shredded spinach to add more veggie to your meal.
- You can alternate cooking oil with 2 TBS of butter.
- Adjust the crushed chilli powder according to your taste.

Tandoori Chicken

Serves: 4

Ingredients:

- 4 pcs. chicken legs/chicken quarters (skinned)
- 3 tablespoons (150ml) full flat yogurt (lightly beaten)
- 2 ½ teaspoon coriander powder
- 2 tablespoons lemon juice
- 2 tablespoons cooking oil
- 1 teaspoon red chili powder
- 1 teaspoon turmeric powder
- 1 teaspoon tandoori masala
- 1 teaspoon ginger garlic paste
- 1 teaspoon garam masala
- 1/8 teaspoon orange red food color (optional)
- 1 ½ tsp salt (or to taste)

Method:

1. Wash and clean the chicken thoroughly.
2. Put the chicken into a bowl and add 1 tablespoon of lemon juice and make deep slashes in each piece. Set aside.
3. Mix together red chili powder, coriander powder, garam masala, tandoori masala, turmeric powder, ginger garlic paste, yogurt, lemon juice, food coloring, cooking oil, and salt.
4. Marinate the chicken for at least an hour in the fridge. Cover and marinate overnight in the refrigerator, if time allows.
5. Preheat the oven to 240 degree.

6. Place the chicken on an oiled grill pan/ shallow oven proof dish and cook in the oven for 25 minutes, turning once until chicken is tender and cooked through.
7. Garnish with sprigs of coriander, lemon wedges and serve with a salad or fried rice.

Mutton Pepper Fry

Serves: 2

Ingredients:

- 200g mutton (boneless)
- 4 pcs cloves
- 3 tablespoons cooking oil (to temper)
- 2 pcs medium-large onions (chopped)
- 2 pcs cardamom pod
- 1 tablespoon ginger garlic paste
- 1 teaspoon fennel seeds
- 1 sprig curry leaves
- 1 teaspoon Turmeric powder
- 1 teaspoon red chili powder
- 1 teaspoon coriander powder
- 1 tablespoon black pepper powder
- ½ inch cinnamon stick

- ½ bunch fresh coriander leaves

To temper:

- 40g cashew nuts
- 3 dry red chili (broken)
- 1 sprig curry leaves

Method:

1. Wash the mutton and cut into small/medium chunks and. Then put them in a bowl.
2. Add 1 teaspoon turmeric powder along with ½ teaspoon of salt and mix well. Set aside for 20 minutes.

3. Heat the oil in a frying pan (or a wok) and add fennel seeds, cinnamon stick, cardamom pod, cloves and curry leaves.
4. Add ginger garlic paste and sauté for 1 minute.
5. Add chopped onion and sauté until onions start to turn brown.
6. Add tomato and sauté for another 1 to 2 minutes.
7. Add all the masala powder (red chili, coriander, turmeric) and sauté for one more minute.
8. Now add the marinated mutton and sauté thoroughly.
9. Add freshly ground black pepper and salt, sauté for about 4 to 5 minutes.
10. Add half cup water and cook the mutton for 30 minutes in a medium flame
11. Stir the mutton well until it becomes slightly dry.
12. Check the taste. Adjust the salt.
13. In the meantime, heat the oil in a small frying pan and add dry red chili, curry leaves and cashew nuts, stir until the cashew starts to turn brown.
14. Remove from the heat and stir the mixture on to mutton
15. Stir in the chopped coriander.
16. Serve hot with rice or paratha.

Spicy Chicken Masala

Serves: 2-3

Ingredients:

- 1 kg chicken skin
- 175 ml thick plain yogurt
- 6 pcs cardamom pods
- 5 pcs cloves
- 5 cloves garlic (chopped)
- 3 tablespoons cooking oil
- 2-inch ginger (chopped)
- 2-inch cinnamon stick
- 2 medium-large tomatoes (chopped)
- 2 medium onion (chopped)
- 1 ½ teaspoon garam masala powder
- 1 sprig curry leaf
- 1 teaspoon turmeric powder
- 1 teaspoon salt (or to taste)
- ½ tablespoon red chili powder

To dry roast:

- 2 tablespoons cumin seeds
- 2 teaspoons coriander seeds
- 3 dry red chilies (or to taste)

Method:

1. Dry roast the cumin, coriander seeds and red chili in a medium-heavy frying pan over a medium heat, stirring them until they turn a few shades darker and give off a

wonderful roasted aroma, about 4 minutes. (Do not let the spices burn)
2. Grind to a fine powder and set aside.
3. Trim off any excess fat or skin from the chicken
4. Mix the ground masala, garam masala, 1 teaspoon of salt and turmeric together and rub it into the chicken.
5. Put half of the onion (or 1 onion), garlic, ginger, and chopped tomatoes in a blender and blend to a smooth paste.
6. Heat oil in a wok add the cloves, cinnamon, cardamom and the remaining onion and fry until the onion is golden brown.
7. Add the tomato and onion paste and stir for 5 minutes.
8. Add the curry leaves and stir with ½ teaspoon of turmeric powder and salt to taste.
9. Add the spiced chicken and stir for 6 to 7 minutes.
10. Stir in the yogurt and bring slowly to boil.
11. Reduce the heat, cover and simmer for 30 minutes or until the oil has separated from the sauce.
12. Stir the ingredients occasionally to prevent the chicken from sticking.
13. Serve hot with plain boiled rice or with any bread.

Amma's Chicken Biryani

Serves: 2

Ingredients:

To marinate the chicken:

- 500 gr chicken (cut into medium size pieces)
- 2 coriander powder
- 1 ½ red chili powder
- ½ teaspoon turmeric powder
- 1 salt

For the biryani rice:

- 2 cups basmati rice
- 3 cups water (to cook rice)
- 3 tablespoons ghee/oil
- 2 tablespoons oil (for chicken)
- 1 cup curd (dilute ½ cup curd with half cup water)
- 1 stick cinnamon
- 1-piece bay leaf
- 2 pcs red onions (slice)
- 2 pcs medium tomatoes (slice)
- 1 green chili (or to taste)
- 1 tablespoon ginger and garlic Paste
- 2 pcs cardamom pods
- 2 pcs cloves
- 1 teaspoon red chili powder
- ½ teaspoon turmeric powder
- ½ teaspoon garam masala

- 1 teaspoon coriander powder
- ½ bunch coriander leaves
- ½ bunch mint leaves
- 1/8 teaspoon kesari powder (optional)
- 1 teaspoon salt (to taste)

Method:

1. Wash the chicken couple of times and marinate with salt, turmeric powder, coriander powder and chili powder. Set aside for 30 minutes.
2. Heat 2 tablespoons of oil in a wok and add marinated chicken the fry for about 6 to 7 minutes until the brown spots appear in the chicken. Set aside.
3. Wash rice and drain.
4. Heat 1 tbs oil/ ghee in a pressure cooker, add cloves, cinnamon, bay leaf and cardamom then fry for 30 seconds.
5. Add ginger garlic paste, green chili along with slice onions and sauté for 2 minutes until onions start to turn brown.
6. Add chopped coriander leaves and mint leaves. Sauté for 30 seconds.
7. Add sliced tomatoes along with chili powder, coriander powder, garam masala powder, turmeric powder and salt. Sauté for 1 minute and then add drained rice.
8. Add cooked chicken and mix well with other spices.
9. Add water and diluted curd mixture and taste the salt.
10. Mix kesari powder with 2 tbs of water and then add to the biryani mixture. Stir in slowly.
11. Mix well and serve hot with raita and with some boiled eggs.

Soya Meat Curry

Serves: 2-3

Ingredients:

- 100 g soya meat
- 40 g onion (slice)
- 3 tablespoons cooking oil
- 2 pcs medium-large tomato (chopped)
- 2 pcs green chili (slice)
- 1 ½ teaspoon salt (or to taste)
- 1 tablespoon chili powder (or to taste)
- 1 tablespoon ginger garlic paste
- 1 teaspoon fennel seeds
- 1 sprig curry leaves
- 1 tablespoon coconut cream
- ½ inch cinnamon stick
- ½ teaspoon turmeric powder

- ½ teaspoon garam masala

- ½ inch torn pandan leaf (optional)

Method:

1. Boil the soya meat in salted hot water for about 5 minutes
2. Once boiled, drain the soya meat and let it cool down for 5 minutes or so.
3. Completely squeeze all the excess water out.
4. Mix the soya meat with turmeric powder, chili powder together with salt and set aside. If the soya meat comes with any flavor you can add the masala mix too. Take care

of the spiciness of the masala and you can adjust the amount of chili powder.
5. Heat the oil in a heavy bottom pan; add the fennel seeds and cinnamon stick.
6. Add the curry leaves, ginger garlic paste, green chili and sliced onions.
7. Sauté for 3 minutes until onions turn translucent.
8. Add tomato and sauté for another 3 minutes until soft.
9. Add marinated soya meat and sauté for 5 minutes until the soya meat become little dry.
10. Splash some water and sauté for another 3 minutes.
11. Add garam masala powder and stir
12. Add little water to just to cover the soya meat and cook for 10 minutes
13. Allow mixture to come to a boil and then reduce the heat.
14. Stir in the coconut milk and cook for further 3 minutes.
15. Serve hot as a side with plain boiled rice or with any flat bread.

Sri Lankan Sour Fish Curry (Ambul Thiyal)

Serves: 4

Ingredients:

- 1kg of black fish (Tuna or Mackerel)
- 8 cardamom pods
- 3 pieces of goroka
- 2 tablespoons cracked black pepper
- 2 green chilies
- 2 cloves garlic
- 1 tablespoon roasted curry powder
- 1 teaspoon salt
- 1 stick of cinnamon
- 1 medium-large onion (finely chopped)
- 1 sprig curry leaves
- 1 tablespoon chili flakes
- 1 slice of ginger
- 1 teaspoon of black pepper corns
- ½ tablespoon coriander
- ½ tablespoon cumin
- ¼ teaspoon fenugreek seeds
- water to cover the fish
- juice of lime

Method:

1. Grind the cardamom pods, coriander, cumin, curry powder, salt, pepper, cinnamon chilies, garlic, chili flakes, ginger, black pepper corns and goroka with a little water onto a grinding stone and make a paste. Set aside.
2. Wash and cut the fish into 4-6 pieces through the bone.

3. Place all the remaining ingredients in earthenware chatty with 250 ml of water and mix until the paste has dissolved.
4. Mix in the fish and then cook over a coal fire, covered, until the water has evaporated.

Pot Roast Yogurt Chicken

Serves: 5

Ingredients:

- 1 whole chicken (cleaned and pat dry with a paper towel)
- 3-4 tablespoons plain yogurt or curd
- 3 tablespoons gee or oil
- 2 medium onion (finely sliced)
- 2 teaspoon chili powder
- 2 cloves garlic (crushed)
- 1 ½ teaspoons salt
- 1 teaspoon Sri Lankan curry powder
- ½ cup of water (or as needed)
- ½ teaspoon ground black peppers
- ¼ teaspoon turmeric powder
- ¼ teaspoon each ground cardamom, cloves, cinnamon and mace (or 1 tsp of biriyani spice mix if you have or put whole if you don't have them powdered)
- oil to deep fry onions.

Method:

1. Mix all the spices, 3 tbs oil, garlic crushed, salt and yogurt in a bowl. Rub the mixture well all over the chicken and put a tbs of the mixture inside the cavity too. Let marinate in the fridge for about 2 hours, best overnight.
2. Deep fry onions until golden brown. Put ½ fried onions inside the cavity of the well marinated chicken.
3. Heat ghee or oil in large heavy pot and put the marinated chicken in breast side down first. Add any leftover

marinade mix on to the chicken (don't waste any of it) and spread the remaining fried onions on the top of the chicken.
4. Cook for about 45 minutes - 1 hour, turning sides and covered with a lid until the chicken is tender and completely cooked. If needed, add a little water time to time to stop it sticking to the pot. Remember if you use a large whole chicken you may need to cook this for longer than an hour. Mine was a medium. To check if the chicken is cooked throughout just cut through the breast with a carving knife and if juices are flowing or if it looks pink, it still needs cooking.
5. Serve hot with rice/salad or with a nice loaf of bread.

Sri Lankan Date Chutney

Serves: 10

Ingredients:

- 500 g pitted dates
- 50 g dried chilies (keep 2-3 aside for dressing)
- 3-4 small cloves of garlic
- 1 tablespoon garlic
- 1 tablespoon ginger
- ½ cup vinegar (I used apple cider vinegar and that was perfect if you can't find Sri Lankan Coconut Vinegar)
- ½ cup sugar (or to your preference)
- salt to taste

Method:

1. Soak dates in hot water for about 2 minutes.
2. Transfer to a blender and blend for 1-2 times. The idea is to break them, not to make a paste.
3. Transfer to a bowl.
4. Add the remaining ingredients in to the blender, except few chilies and whole garlic.
5. Make a nice marinade like paste. Transfer to dates.
6. Add remaining whole chilies and garlic and mix all well together.
7. Chutneys and pickles always taste better next day.
8. Transfer to a jar and seal with a lid. You can keep this outside up to a week.
9. This goes well with rice and curries or with Biryani.

Grilled Spicy Squids

Serves: 3

Ingredients:

- 3 medium- large whole squids (cleaned)
- 2 tablespoons oil
- 1 tablespoon chili flakes
- 1 tablespoon chili powder
- 1 tablespoon sugar/maple syrup/honey
- 1 teaspoon of garlic and ginger
- 1 teaspoon mustard paste
- 1 teaspoon soy sauce
- salt to taste

Method:

1. Score the squids only on one side (so it is still a whole squid not separated in to rings).
2. Mix all the ingredients, except the oil and make a nice thick paste. Dip the squids in one by one and get them nicely coated with the paste.
3. Heat a grill pan with oil (you can also cook this on the BBQ). Once the oil is heated, transfer coated squids on to the pan. Cook both sides for about 4 minutes each brushing the remaining marinate mix on the squid. Transfer to a plate and garnish with sliced spring onions.
4. Serve with steamed rice or with a salad.

Tip:

- Use a weight to stop the squids from curling up while cooking. (I used a Pyrex dish) As soon as the squids are transferred to the hot pans put the Pyrex dish to keep them touching the pan and when turn over, do the same.

Claypot Dark Chicken and Egg Rice

Serves: 3

Ingredients:

For the Dark chicken curry:

- 4 pieces of chicken thigh cutlets with bones.
- 1-inch piece of pandan leaves
- 2-3 tablespoons of oil
- 2 teaspoon chili powder (use paprika for a mild curry)
- 2 tablespoons vinegar
- 2 tablespoons soy sauce
- 2 garlic cloves (sliced)
- 1 ½ tablespoons dark roasted Sri Lankan curry powder
- 1 onion (sliced)
- 1 teaspoon ginger
- 1 teaspoon fenugreek seeds
- ¼ cup water
- sprig of curry leaves
- piece of cinnamon
- salt and pepper to taste

For the rice:

- 2 cups of basmati rice (washed and drained)
- 3 medium-large eggs (hardboiled)
- 1 onion (cut into chunks)
- 2 green chilies (chopped)
- ¼ cup of thick coconut milk

- salt to taste

Method:

1. Marinade chicken with salt, pepper, vinegar, curry powder and soy sauce and set aside. (leave in the fridge over night for best results).
2. Heat oil in a pan and add fenugreek seeds, curry leaves, pandan leaves, garlic and ginger. Cook for about a minute and then add chili powder and cook for another 30 seconds on low heat. Add onions and green chilies. Mix well and add marinated chicken after another minute. Cover with a lid and cook for five minutes on low heat. After 5 minutes turn chicken over and cook for another 5 minutes on low. Then add water and turn heat up to medium and cook for another 20-30 minutes (stirring occasionally) or until the chicken is completely cooked.
3. Layer washed rice on the top of chicken, add enough water to cook rice (this will depend on the type of rice you cook with). Insert boiled eggs into rice and cover well with rice. Cover with a lid, and on high heat bring water to boil. Then reduce the heat and cook until all the water evaporates and rice cooked. (That is how you cook perfect rice on the stove).
4. Once the rice is cooked add all the remaining ingredients and salt to taste and cook for a minute or two.
5. Serve immediately. I complimented this dish with a delicious Malay pickle.

Tip:

- Take out the boiled eggs before you mix well to prevent them from breaking.

Chapter Three: Sri Lankan Dinner Recipes

Crab Curry with Roasted Coconut

Serves: 4

Ingredients:

- 4-6 medium-large crab (cleaned)
- 3-4 tablespoons coconut (fresh scraped or defrosted frozen/dry desiccated / shredded coconut for anyone who cannot source fresh)
- 3-4 garlic cloves (chopped)
- 2-3 green chilies
- 2-3 tablespoons oil
- 2 sprigs of curry leaves
- 1 cup thick coconut milk
- 1 medium onion (chopped)
- 1 medium tomato (chopped)
- 1 tablespoon rice
- 1 tablespoon chili flakes
- 1 ½ teaspoon of Sri Lankan curry powder
- 1 teaspoon chili powder
- 1 teaspoon fenugreek seed
- 1 teaspoon mustard
- 1 teaspoon pepper powder
- 1 teaspoon ginger paste
- pandan leaf
- cinnamon stick
- ½ cup water
- salt to taste

Method:

1. Roast the coconut and rice individually until golden brown and set aside.
2. Heat oil in a large pan (big enough for all your crabs to go in) and add garlic, ginger, curry leaves, pandan leaf, mustard seeds, cinnamon, cook for about 30 seconds until they start releasing flavors and fragrant smell.
3. Then add green chilies, chopped onion and chopped tomato. Let them all cook for about 2 minutes. Add chili powder, curry powder, chili flakes, cleaned crabs, salt and pepper. Mix well and let cook for another 2 minutes in medium to high heat. Then add water and let cook for about 15 minutes.
4. In the meantime, using a blender or motor and pestle grind roasted coconut and rice together adding a little water. Add this mixture to coconut milk. After 15-minute mark, add this to the crab cook for another 10 15 minutes. Check for salt and pepper and garnish with coriander.
5. Serve with rice or fresh bread.

Dal Methi

Serves: 2-3

Ingredients:

- 1 teaspoon mustard seeds
- ½ cup split chickpeas
- mustard seeds
- 1 garlic cloves (chopped)
- Fenugreek seeds
- Red chili powder
- Turmeric powder
- Grated jaggery
- Tamarind juice
- Salt
- Oil
- Coriander

Method:

1. Soak the fenugreek seeds and split peas for a few hours.
2. Cook it in the pressure cooker.
3. Heat oil in a pan and add mustard seeds and garlic.
4. After stir frying, add turmeric and red chili powder.
5. Then add the cooked lentils and pour some water.
6. Add tamarind juice and cook for some time.
7. Finally, add the chopped coriander leaves.
8. This will go nicely with warm rice.

Aloo Gobi

Serves: 2

Ingredients:

- 2 medium-large potatoes (sliced or cubed)
- 3-4 teaspoons oil
- 2 tablespoons chopped cilantro
- 2 medium tomatoes (chopped)
- 1 ½ teaspoons ginger-garlic paste
- 1 medium cauliflower (cut into small florets)
- 1 teaspoon coriander powder
- 1 medium onion (chopped)
- ½ teaspoon cumin seeds
- ½ teaspoon turmeric powder
- ½ teaspoon dry mango powder (amchur)
- ¼ teaspoon red chili powder (or to taste)
- ¼ teaspoon garam masala powder
- salt to taste

Method:

1. Heat 2 teaspoon of oil in a pan on medium heat. Add cauliflower florets and fry for about 2-3 minutes and then add the sliced potatoes.
2. Fry on low-medium flame for 7-8 minutes till potatoes and cauliflower have some brown spots on them.
3. Drain on a tissue paper to remove excess oil and set aside.
4. In the same pan, heat 1 ½ teaspoon of oil on medium heat and add cumin seeds and let them crackle.
5. Add the onions and cook for 2 minutes till translucent.

6. Add the ginger-garlic paste and cook for another 2 minutes or till the raw smell goes away.
7. Add the chopped tomatoes and cook for 2 minutes till they are little soft.
8. Add turmeric powder, red chili powder, coriander powder and amchur (mango powder).
9. Cover the pan and let the masala cook for 2-3 minutes and then add the potatoes and cauliflower to it and mix.
10. Add chopped coriander leaves and give a good mix.
11. Add garam masala and cook the potato and cauliflower on medium-low heat for 5-6 minutes.
12. Add salt and cover the pan and cook more additional 6-7 minutes on low flame or till the potato and cauliflower are tender but not soggy. If you feel the masala is sticking, you may add some water. Add 1 tablespoon at a time and only add enough to cook the veggies. I did not add any water in mine.
13. Garnish with some more coriander leaves and serve hot with any Indian bread.

Peter Kuruvita's Beetroot Curry

Serves: 6

Ingredients:

- 350 g (12 oz) small beetroots (washed & trimmed)
- 200 ml (7 fl oz) coconut milk
- 50 g (1 ¾ oz) ghee
- 3 cm piece pandan leaf
- 2 garlic cloves (thinly sliced)
- 2 small-medium green chilies (finely chopped)
- 1 large onion (finely chopped)
- 1 sprig curry leaves (leaves picked)
- 1 cinnamon stick
- 3 teaspoons white vinegar
- 1 teaspoon ground coriander
- 1 teaspoon chili powder
- 1 teaspoon caster sugar

Method:

1. If you are using the beetroots, cut and stems into 1cm (1/2 in) pieces.
2. Heat the ghee in a heavy-based saucepan over medium heat and cook the onion and green chili for 6-8 minutes or until translucent. Add the pandan leaf, curry leaves and garlic and cook for another 3 minutes or until fragrant.
3. Add the remaining ingredients, cover, and simmer over very low heat, stirring occasionally for 15-20 minutes or until the beetroot is tender.
4. Season to taste and serve.

Sri Lankan Style Vegetable Fried Rice

Serves: 6-7

Ingredients:

- 5 cups Basmati rice (washed, soaked in water for 15 minutes and drained)
- 6 cups vegetable stock or water
- 2 medium-large eggs
- 1 medium-large carrot (peeled and cut into thin matchsticks)
- 1 leek (green part only, cut into thin matchsticks)
- 1 small onion (chopped finely)
- 1 teaspoon garlic and ginger paste
- a handful of green peas (thawed)
- a large knob of butter
- 2 teaspoon oil
- a few curry leaves

Method:

1. Heat half of the oil and butter in a large frying pan (or a wok) and sauté the curry leaves and then add the onions. Stir and fry untill onions are translucent.
2. Add the drained rice and stir fry over low heat for another 5 minutes.
3. Add the stock or water and cook, either in a rice cooker if you have one or on the stove, on high heat until most of the water evaporates.
4. Then cover and lower the heat to very low and cook covered and without peeking for another 15 minutes or till rice is done. Leave to cool.
5. Heat the rest of the oil and butter in wok.

6. Then add the ginger garlic paste and fry for a few seconds and add the finely cut carrots and leeks and stir fry. Add the peas.
7. Then add the cold rice and stir fry till combined.
8. Make a thin omelet with the two eggs and salt and pepper.
9. Cut into thin strips and decorate the rice with it.
10. Serve while hot.

Seer Fish in Vinegar and Mustard Sauce

Serves: 3-4

Ingredients:

- 500 gm seer fish or any white fish such as king fish
- 5 cloves of garlic (thinly sliced)
- 5 cm piece of ginger (grated finely)
- 2 tablespoons white vinegar
- 2 medium onions (sliced into rounds)
- 1 teaspoon ground mustard seeds
- 1 teaspoon ground black pepper
- 1 tablespoon oil
- 1 teaspoon salt
- ½ teaspoon turmeric
- ½ cup of coconut milk
- a few curry leaves
- a couple of pieces of pandan leaves (rampe)
- a few peppercorns
- 2-3 pieces of gamboge or goraka (optional)
- a handful of chopped coriander leaves/cilantro (optional)

Method:

1. Start by cutting the fish into portion size. Place the fish slices in a saucepan and sprinkle a little water.
2. Add the pandan, gamboge and curry leaves, turmeric, peppercorns, salt to taste and cook on low heat until the fish is partly cooked. Leave a side.
3. Heat oil in a large frying pan or wok. Add some curry leaves and sauté. Add the onion rings, green chilies and sliced garlic and ginger and stir fry till soft but now

brown. Then add the liquid from the fish and coconut milk and cook until thick.
4. Add the mustard, salt and pepper. Add the fish pieces making sure you don't break them and mix until the fish is nicely coated and done.
5. Serve in a shallow dish with the onion and sauce covering the fish pieces.

Sri Lankan Pork Badun Curry (Deviled Pork)

Serves: 4

Ingredients:

- 2 pounds pork (cut into cubes, bone-in pieces are fine too)
- 20 curry leaves
- 6 green cardamom pods
- 6 cloves
- 5 garlic cloves (minced or grated, 1 heaping tablespoon)
- 4 tablespoons canola oil (divided)
- 3 tablespoons curry powder (roasted, I used Sri Lankan curry powder)
- 3 teaspoons tamarind paste
- 2 inches ginger (minced or grated, 1 heaping tablespoon)
- 2 tablespoons red chili powder
- 2 pieces pandan leaves
- 1 ½ cups water
- 1 stalk lemongrass (bruised and cut into 1-inch pieces)
- 1 teaspoon fenugreek seeds
- 1 (1 inch) cinnamon stick
- 1 medium onion (chopped)
- 1 tablespoon vinegar
- 1 cup coconut milk
- salt (to taste, salt dish throughout cooking process)

Method:

1. Heat 2-3 tablespoons canola oil in a large pan on medium heat. Add curry leaves, pandan leaves, lemongrass, fenugreek seeds, cinnamon stick, green cardamom pods and cloves. Fry for about 1-2 minutes. Then add chopped onion, some salt and ginger/garlic and sauté for 2-3 minutes.
2. Increase heat to medium-high, then add the cubed pork and sauté with all ingredients in pan for 2-3 minutes. Next add the curry powder, salt and chili powder and sauté for 3-5 minutes.
3. Once the meat and spices are well browned add the tamarind paste, vinegar and water and pour into curry.
4. Lower the heat down to medium and allow curry to simmer for 30 minutes with a lid on the pot. Stir it occasionally. After the meat has finished cooking, heat 1 tablespoon of canola oil on high heat in a separate pan.
5. Add all the pieces of pork to the oil and fry them. Avoid putting the gravy in the 2nd pan with the oil. Fry the pork for 3-5 minutes until browned.
6. Add the fried pork back into the curry pan with the gravy and the coconut milk. Bring to a simmer for 3-4 minutes, taste for seasoning and serve with rice and curries or Indian flat breads. Enjoy.

Note:

- Roasted curry powder is curry powder that is gently toasted in a pan until fragrant and dark. Sri Lankan roasted curry powder is best for this dish.

Sri Lankan Sates

Serves: 48

Ingredients:

Chicken:

- 1 ½ pound boneless skinless chicken breast halves
- 3 tablespoons vegetable oil
- 2 cloves garlic (minced)
- 2 teaspoons ground coriander
- 1 tablespoon paprika (hot or sweet)
- 1 teaspoon salt to taste
- 1 teaspoon freshly ground black pepper

Sauce:

- 1 cup coconut milk (canned or homemade)
- 1 medium-large onion (thinly sliced)
- 2 cloves garlic (minced)
- 3 tablespoons vegetable oil
- 2 teaspoons white vinegar (distilled or more to taste)
- 1 tablespoon fresh ginger (minced)
- 1 teaspoon ground cumin
- 1 teaspoon ground coriander
- ½ teaspoon paprika (hot or cayenne pepper)
- ½ teaspoon ground turmeric
- salt and freshly ground black pepper to taste

Method:

1. Rinse the chicken breasts under cold running water, then drain and blot dry with paper towels. Cut the breasts

lengthwise (with the grain) into 2 1/2-inch-long strips and place in a large bowl. Add the paprika, coriander, salt, and pepper, and garlic rubbing into the meat with your fingers.
2. Stir in the oil to coat thoroughly, cover, and let marinate, in the refrigerator, for 30 minutes or up to 6 hours (the longer the better).
3. Meanwhile, prepare the sauce. Heat the oil in a medium-size saucepan over high heat. Add the onion, ginger, garlic, cumin, coriander, 1/2 teaspoon paprika, the turmeric, and salt and black pepper. Sauté for 1 minute, stirring to coat the onion with the seasonings.
4. Reduce the heat to medium and cook the onion, stirring occasionally, until very soft and a deep golden brown, 15 to 20 minutes.
5. Stir in the coconut milk and 2 teaspoons vinegar. Simmer until you have a thick, spoon able sauce, about 5 minutes. Taste for seasoning, adding salt or vinegar as necessary; the mixture should be highly seasoned. Remove from the heat and set aside.
6. Preheat the grill to high.
7. Weave the chicken strips lengthwise onto the skewers.
8. When ready to cook, oil the grill grate. Arrange the sates on the hot grate and grill, turning with tongs, until lightly browned and cooked through, 1 to 3 minutes per side (2 to 6 minutes in all).
9. Transfer the sates to serving plates or a platter and spoon a little sauce over each. Serve immediately.

Sri Lankan Coconut Dhal with Crispy Onions

Serves: 4

Ingredients:

Dhal:

- 400ml coconut milk
- 10 fresh curry leaves
- 3 cloves of garlic (crushed)
- 1 1/2 cups of red lentils
- 1 onion (diced)
- 1 teaspoon turmeric
- 1 teaspoon curry powder
- 1 cinnamon quill

Crunchy onions:

- 15 curry leaves
- 5 shallots (sliced)
- 3 cloves of garlic (sliced)
- 1 teaspoon mustard seeds
- ¼ cup coconut oil
- coriander leaves and limes to serve

Method:

1. Rinse and drain the lentils really well then add to a large pot along with the all the dhal ingredients and 350ml of water. Bring to a boil then reduce to a low simmer for 20-25 minutes or until the lentils are soft. Keep an eye on it in case you want to add more water.

2. In the meantime, heat the coconut oil in a nonstick pan and add the onion ingredients. Stir until golden and crunchy then turn off the heat.
3. Once the lentils are tender and mushy, season well with salt then serve with rice, coriander and drizzle over the crunchy onion mixture.

Sri Lankan Shrimp Curry

Serves: 4

Ingredients:

- 1 lb. medium-large shrimp (cleaned)
- 3-5 cloves of garlic (finely chopped)
- 2 inches of ginger (grated)
- 1 (2 inch) stick of cinnamon
- 1 medium onion (chopped)
- 1-2 chili peppers (sliced)
- 2 tablespoons of lemon juice
- 1 cup coconut milk
- 1 teaspoon of fenugreek seeds
- ½ cup of water
- ½ teaspoon of turmeric
- handful of curry leaves
- 1 tablespoon of red chili powder (or to taste)
- salt to taste
- 1 stalk of lemon grass (pounded a few times) optional

Method:

1. You can use frozen or fresh shrimp (do not use already cooked shrimp). I used frozen shrimp that I defrosted under cold water. My shrimp was cleaned with only the tails on. I do think that the shrimp shells give a wonderful flavor to the gravy so if you don't mind cleaning your shrimp as you eat, the shells are good to have while you cook the dish.

2. Add all the ingredients to the pan and bring to a simmer on medium-high heat. You will see more liquid form in the pan from the shrimp.
3. Simmer for 10 minutes with the lid on. Stir occasionally.
4. Add coconut milk and stir well.
5. Taste for salt here. Eat with rice other curries. Enjoy.

Sri Lankan Meatball Curry

Serves: 4

Ingredients:

For the meatballs:

- 2 lb. of your favorite lean ground meat (chicken, beef, pork)
- 2-3 slices of bread soaked in milk to soften
- 1 tablespoon ginger (grated)
- 1 tablespoon garlic (grated)
- 1 tablespoon paprika
- 1 medium-large egg
- salt and pepper to taste

For the meatball curry:

- 15oz can of diced tomatoes
- 10-20 curry leaves
- 2-3 cloves
- 2-3 green cardamom pods
- 2 serrano or jalapeno chilies (seeded and chopped)
- 2 tablespoons of grated ginger
- 1 large onion (chopped)
- 1 small (1 inch) cinnamon stick
- 1 teaspoon fennugreek seeds
- 1 tablespoon of grated garlic
- 1 cup of coconut milk
- 1 cup of water
- 1 teaspoon vinegar
- 1 tablespoon of chili/cayenne powder (or to taste)
- 1-2 tablespoon of curry powder (to taste)

- ½ teaspoon of turmeric
- salt to taste
- 1-2 pandan leaves (optional)

Method:

1. Form the meatballs into any size you like. Shallow fry them (on medium-high heat) until all the sides are browned in about 2 tablespoons of canola oil. You don't have to cook them all the way through because they will finish cooking in the gravy. Once fried, place them on a plate until the gravy is made.
2. In the same pan you fried the meatballs with, use the oil that is left to fry the curry leaves, cinnamon stick, cardamoms, cloves, pandan leaves, onions, and green chilies for about a minute on medium high heat.
3. Next the ginger, garlic and season with some salt. Then add the curry powder, red chili powder and turmeric to bloom the spices for a minute.
4. Next add diced tomatoes (you can substitute 2-3 fresh tomatoes as well), vinegar, water and meatballs to pan. Simmer for 15 minutes.
5. Finally add coconut milk and simmer for another 2-3 minutes. Taste for salt and seasoning.
6. Enjoy with rice, vegetable curries, lentils or fried rice.

Sri Lankan Black Pepper Chicken Curry.

Serves: 4

Ingredients:

- 500g of chicken (can include legs and other parts)
- 4 tablespoons of oil
- 3 cardamom pods
- 2 tablespoons of pepper (start with 1 tablespoon and add more as per your taste)
- 2-3 tablespoons of tamarind juice (1 tablespoon of tamarind soaked in 1/4 water for 5 minutes)
- 2 whole green chilies
- 1 tablespoon of garlic and ginger paste (3 cloves and a 1-inch piece of ginger can be minced for this purpose)
- 1 large onion (finely sliced)
- 1-inch cinnamon piece
- 1 medium-large tomato (sliced into four)
- 1 teaspoon cumin powder
- 1 teaspoon coriander powder
- 1 cup coconut milk
- 1/2 teaspoon of turmeric powder
- a handful of curry leaves
- a 2-inch piece of pandan leaf
- salt to season

Method:

1. Wash, clean and place the chicken parts in a bowl, add one 1/2 teaspoon of salt, tamarind juice, mix and let it sit while you prepare the curry.

2. Over medium heat, place a cooking pan and pour in the oil, once the oil heats (1 minute), add the curry leaves, pandan leaf, cardamom, cinnamon followed by ginger-garlic paste. cook for a minute before adding the onions, green chilies and tomatoes.
3. Sauté the ingredients over low-medium heat until onions and tomatoes turn soft. 5-7 minutes.
4. Reduce heat and add the chicken (with the marinade) to the cooking pan
5. Add turmeric, cumin, coriander, pepper over the chicken and while the heat is low, mix all the ingredients in the pan for 2-3 minutes.
6. Cover and let the curry simmer for 5-7 minutes until there is no liquid if you prefer to fry the chicken at this stage add 2 tablespoons of oil and let the chicken brown slightly OR continue to cook until all liquid evaporates and proceed to next stage.
7. Pour in the coconut milk, reduce heat, season with salt if necessary then cover and simmer until gravy thickens and takes on a darker hue.15-25 minutes.
8. Serve warm with your favorite rice and curry dishes.

Sri Lankan Rice and Chicken Congee (Kanji)

Serves: 4

Ingredients:

- 500g-700g chicken breast
- 250g carrots (cleaned and shredded into thin slivers)
- 10 cloves of garlic
- 4 pieces of long pandan leaves
- 3 cups of water
- 2-3 pieces of cinnamon
- 2 teaspoons of fenugreek seeds
- 2 tablespoons of oil
- 1 medium-large onion
- 1 cup of rice
- 1 cup of thick milk
- ½ teaspoon of turmeric

For the coconut chutney/paste(thovayal)-this should be made extra spicy:

- 5 cloves of garlic
- 3 shallots (not bombay onions)
- 2 teaspoons of chili flakes
- 2 teaspoon of tamarind juice
- 2 green chilies
- 1 cup of grated coconut
- 1 teaspoon minced ginger
- salt to season

Method:

Making the coconut chutney/paste(thovayal):

1. Place all the ingredient in a grinder and blitz until you have a fine paste, season with salt if necessary, place it in a container and refrigerate until you use. You can also make extra and refrigerate but use it within three days.

Making the rice and chicken kanji(congee):

1. Have all the ingredients prepared and ready to make the kanji(congee).
2. Wash the rice and chicken breast (the whole chicken) and set aside.
3. Use a large pan, as the volume of the congee increases when the rice is cooked and coconut milk is added.
4. Place the pan over medium heat and pour in the oil, add the sliced onions, turmeric, pandan leaves, cinnamon and shredded carrots.
5. Cook for 2-3 minutes until all the ingredients turn soft while the onion slightly brown.
6. Pour in water, add garlic, fenugreek seed and chicken breast into the pan (see notes above on adding chicken to the kanji). season with salt and cook over medium heat.
7. Pour in water, add garlic, fenugreek seed and chicken breast into the pan (see notes above on adding chicken to the kanji). season with salt and cook over medium heat.
8. Once you've removed the chicken breast from the pan, let it cool for a few minutes then shred (if it is still hot use two forks to do this quickly).
9. Add the shredded chicken to the cooking rice and let it simmer until water is reduced by half. using a wooden spoon mash the rice a little to break the grains.
10. Pour in thin coconut milk and slow-simmer over low heat for 15 minutes, followed by thick coconut milk, once you

add coconut milk (both thin and thick), at no point should you let it boil but continue to slow-simmer over low heat for another 10 minutes. check for seasoning of salt and immediately remove the pan from direct heat or the porridge will continue to cook in the remaining heat and thicken.
11. If you find the porridge still too thick, pour 1/2 cup of water.
12. Add thovayal or deep-fried and seasoned onions and garlic crispies.
13. Serve warm.

Sri Lankan Beef Smore

Serves: 4-6

Ingredients:

- One 2 ½ pound piece of beef (shoulder meat, tied as a roast, or a piece of chuck, or even brisket—any beef chunk suitable for braising)
- 4 teaspoons whole coriander seeds
- 4 cloves garlic (finely chopped)
- 4 tablespoons olive or canola oil
- 2 tablespoons red wine vinegar
- 1 ½ cups beef or chicken stock
- 1 large onion (finely chopped)
- 1 teaspoon whole cumin seeds
- 1 teaspoon whole fennel seeds
- 1 cup coconut milk
- 1 2-inch cinnamon stick
- 1 2-inch piece fresh ginger (peeled and finely grated)
- ¼ teaspoon whole fenugreek seeds
- ½ to 1 teaspoon cayenne pepper
- salt to taste
- freshly ground black pepper

Method:

1. Pat the meat dry and sprinkle lightly with salt and lots of black pepper.
2. Set a small cast-iron or other heavy frying pan over medium heat. When very hot, sprinkle in the coriander, cumin, fennel, and fenugreek seeds. Stir for 30 seconds or so until the spices just start to emit a roasted aroma.

Empty onto a piece of paper towel, and, when cooled off a bit, grind the spices in a clean coffee grinder or crush in a mortar.
3. Preheat oven to 325°F.
4. Pour the oil into an ovenproof casserole-type pan and set over medium high heat. When hot, put in the meat and brown on all sides. Remove to a plate. Add the cinnamon, onions, ginger, and garlic. Stir and cook 4 to 5 minutes.
5. Add the vinegar, stock, cayenne, 1 1/2 teaspoons salt, and the beef as well as its accumulated juices. Bring to a boil, stirring the sauce. Cover and place in oven. Cook, basting and turning every 20 minutes or so, about 2 to 2 1/2 hours or until meat is tender. Remove pan from oven. Add the coconut milk, stir, and bring to a simmer before serving.

Sri Lankan Vegetable Curry

Serves: 4-6

Ingredients:

- 1 ½ pounds yams or orange flesh sweet potatoes (peeled and cut into 1-inch cubes)
- 8 whole cloves
- 6 cups of cauliflower florets
- 4 tablespoons cooking oil or ghee (divided)
- 3 hot green chili peppers (divided). 2 sliced in half lengthwise, 1 thinly sliced crosswise. Or double the chilies if you want to kick up the heat
- 2 yellow onions (divided, one sliced, one chopped)
- 2 teaspoons brown or black mustard seeds
- 2 sprigs of fresh curry leaves (divided)
- 2 tablespoons Indian curry powder (such as Madras)
- 2 tablespoons minced garlic (divided)
- 1 tablespoon plus 1 teaspoon minced fresh ginger (divided)
- 1 ½ cups water
- 1 13 ½ ounce can unsweetened coconut milk (shaken well before opening)
- 1 3-inch cinnamon stick (broken in half)
- 1 teaspoon kosher salt
- ¾ pound green beans (stem end trimmed off)
- ½ teaspoon ground turmeric
- salt and fresh ground black pepper to taste

Method:

Make the curry:

1. Heat 2 tablespoons oil or ghee in a large heavy pot or dutch oven over medium heat. Add sliced onion, 1 tablespoon of the garlic, 1 tablespoon of the ginger, the two halved chilies, cinnamon, cloves and one sprig of curry leaves (about 7 leaves). Sauté everything, stirring frequently, about 4 minutes, until the onion starts to soften and everything is fragrant. Add curry powder, turmeric and salt. Cook, stirring, for one minute longer, until fragrant.
2. Add sweet potatoes, water and ½ cup coconut milk. Cook for a minute or two, stirring with a wooden spoon, and coating the sweet potatoes, until the water starts to simmer. Add cauliflower and green beans. Stir, to coat, as you bring the pot to a boil. Turn heat down to a simmer. Cover and cook for 10 minutes, stirring occasionally, until the vegetables are just tender. Add the rest of the coconut milk and cook, uncovered, for a minute or so, until hot. Season, to taste, with salt and pepper. Remove from heat.

Finishing:

1. Heat remaining 2 tablespoons oil or ghee in a small skillet over medium heat. Add the chopped onion, the thinly sliced chili, the remaining 1 tablespoon garlic, the remaining 1 teaspoon ginger, mustard seeds, and 1 sprig of curry leaves. Cook, stirring frequently, for 5 minutes or so, until the onion starts to brown.
2. Stir the onion mixture through the finished curry or ladle the curry into bowls and spoon the mixture on top. Sprinkle with cilantro leaves and toasted cashews.
3. Serve curry with white or brown rice or naan.

Note:

- Remove cinnamon sticks. Curry leaves are edible but you might want to remove any that aren't softened into the curry.

Chapter Four: Sri Lankan Dessert Recipes

Jaggery Chip Coconut Cookies

Serves: 6

Ingredients:

- ½ cup flour
- ¼ cup jaggery chips
- ¼ cup coconut (freshly scraped and toasted)
- ¼ cup butter
- vanilla essence

Method:

1. Mix the flour and butter.
2. Add the jaggery chips, toasted coconut and vanilla.
3. Chill the dough for 15 to 30 mins.
4. Slice dough and bake at 180C for around 15 – 20 mins.
5. Serve with a cup of Sri Lankan tea.

Rava Kesari

Serves: 3-4

Ingredients:

- 10 roasted cashew nuts (roughly chopped)
- 2 cups sugar
- 2 cups water
- 1 cup semolina/rava
- 1 teaspoon cardamom powder
- ¼ cup ghee
- 1/8 teaspoon kesari powder or orange organic coloring.

Method:

1. Start by dry roasting the semolina with 1 teaspoon of ghee in a pan (or a wok).
2. In the same pan, add 1 teaspoon of ghee and roast the cashew nuts until golden brown. Then add 2 cups of water.
3. When the water starts to boil, add roasted semolina and mix without any lumps.
4. When the semolina is cooked, add 2 cups of sugar and stir well.
5. Meanwhile, add kesari powder and cardamom powder and mix everything until well combined.
6. Add ¼ cup of ghee and cook the mixture until thick.
7. Add roasted cashew nuts and cook until the kesari mixture starts to leave the pan.
8. Transfer the mixture onto a buttered dish and cut into desired sizes.
9. Serve warm

Note:

- You can use saffron thread instead of kesari powder. Soak a few strands of saffron threads in the warm milk add it to keasri mixture.

Corn Flour Muskat/Halwa

Serves: 3-4

Ingredients:

- 155g corn flour
- 250g sugar
- 25 roasted cashews (broken into pieces)
- 3 tablespoons ghee
- 1/8 teaspoon kesari powder/orange food coloring
- water (to make smooth paste)
- ½ teaspoon ghee/butter (for greasing the pan & to roast the cashew nuts)

Method:

1. Roast the cashew nuts with little butter until evenly brown and set aside.
2. In a mixing bowl put the corn flour, sugar and coloring powder and mix well.
3. Add enough water to make a smooth paste.
4. And mix until well combined and make sure there are no lumps formed.
5. Pour the mixture in a heavy based pan.
6. Cook the mixture over medium flame.
7. When the mixture starts to thick reduce the flame to low and keep stirring.
8. Once the mixture starts to leave the pan add the ghee. Adding ghee will give nice aroma and glossy finish.
9. Pour the mixture into the greased pan.
10. Spread out to an even thickness.
11. Let it cool for some time.

12. Once cool enough to touch, cut the muskat into diamonds/squares or any shapes that you prefer.

1 Minute Eggless Chocolate Brownie

Serves: 1

Ingredients:

- 2 tablespoons plain flour
- 2 tablespoons fresh milk
- 1 ½ tablespoons sugar
- 2 teaspoons cocoa powder
- ¼ teaspoon baking powder
- ¼ teaspoon vanilla essence
- ¼ teaspoon canola oil
- a pinch of salt

Method:

1. In a microwave safe bowl, mix flour, sugar, baking powder, cocoa powder and salt.
2. Add milk, vanilla extract and oil.
3. Mix well until well combined.
4. Microwave on high for about one minute.
5. Insert a skewer gently in the brownie to check if it's done.
6. If skewer did not come out clean, microwave for another 10 seconds.
7. Enjoy with a glass of milk.

Sri Lankan Rulang Aluwa

Serves: 2-3

Ingredients:

- 200g semolina/rulang
- 130g grated fresh coconut
- 210ml kithul treacle
- 2 tablespoons sugar
- 40g cashew nuts
- ½ teaspoon cardamom powder
- 1 teaspoon ghee
- ¼ teaspoon salt

Method:

1. In a non-stick pan, over medium heat, dry roast the semolina until light brown in color. Keep stirring so it doesn't burn. Set aside.
2. In a same pan dry roast the coconut until brown in color and set aside.
3. Using the same pan add the ghee and roast the cashew nuts until golden. Set aside.
4. In a medium pan add the sugar, kithul treacle, cardamom powder and salt. Cook the mixture on a medium heat until sugar dissolved, meanwhile add the roasted coconut and stir well.
5. When the mixture starts to boil add the roasted semolina and roasted cashews, mix until well combined. When the mixture starts to leave the pan, immediately transfer onto the greased sheet pan and flatten with heated banana leaf/back of your spatula.
6. Cut into square or diamond shape with buttered knife.
7. Serve while hot.

Chocolate Swiss Roll Cake

Serves: 2-3

Ingredients:

- 75 g plain flour
- 30 g cocoa powder
- 100g caster/fine sugar
- 3 medium-large eggs (room temperature)
- 1 ½ tablespoons hot water

Chocolate butter cream:

- 75 g butter
- 175 g icing sugar
- 1 tablespoon cocoa powder
- 1 teaspoon milk

Method:

1. Preheat the oven to 200°/ fan oven 180°C, Line a swiss roll tin with nonstick baking parchment.
2. Crack the eggs in a bowl and using the electric beaters beat the eggs for about 2 minutes.
3. Add the sugar and beat until very pale and fluffy. This will take about 5-6 minutes.
4. Sift together the flour and cocoa powder.
5. Gently fold the flour mixture into the egg mixture. Pour the boiling water and mix gently using a metal spoon until almost combined.
6. Now spread the mixture into the prepared tin.
7. Tap sheet lightly on counter to pop any large air bubbles.
8. Bake in the oven for 8-10 minutes until surface is puffed and springy to touch.

9. Remove the tin from the oven and let it cool for 2 minutes.
10. Turn the sponge out on to wire rack/board carefully peel away parchment.
11. Place a large kitchen towel (you can use fresh sheet of baking parchment) and flip cake over so towel side is underneath.
12. Starting to one long side, gently roll up warm cake inside towel.
13. Let cake cool. Seam side down about half an hour.

For the filling:

1. Meanwhile, prepare the chocolate butter cream by whisking butter and icing sugar along with cocoa powder.
2. Beat until smooth and creamy.
3. Add the milk and beat again until smooth and fluffy consistency.
4. Once the roll is cool enough, carefully unroll towel and cake on a flat surface (cake will curl at the ends and may have a few small cracks)
5. Spread the chocolate butter cream and then re-roll it, keeping towel on exterior.
6. Chill, seam down about 30 minutes. Sift over some icing sugar and serve.

Ultimate Ginger Toffee

Serves: 4-5

Ingredients:

- 400 g full cream condensed milk
- ½ tin sugar (measure in the same tin)
- 1 tablespoon freshly grated ginger
- 50g cashew nuts (roasted & broken into small pieces)
- 1 tablespoon butter

Method:

1. Heat a medium size heavy pan and add the condensed milk.
2. Add the sugar and ginger.
3. Cook in a medium flame until sugar completely dissolves in the mixture.
4. Add the butter and cook the mixture for about 5 minutes.
5. Once the mixture starts to boil, add the roasted cashew nuts.
6. Keep stirring the mixture for 15 minutes or until the mixture is light golden color and starts to leave the pan.
7. Spread the mixture evenly into a greased flat pan.
8. After about 20 minutes, cut into squares.
9. Serve.

Milk (Maid) Peda

Serves: 4-5

Ingredients:

- 400 g Sweetened Condensed Milk (Milkmaid Tin)
- 4 tablespoons milk powder (plus ¼ cup)
- 2 teaspoons lime juice
- 1 ½ teaspoon corn flour
- 1 ½ tablespoons ghee
- ½ cup full cream milk

Method:

1. Mix the milk maid and milk together.
2. Add 4 tablespoons of milk powder, corn flour, ghee and lime juice.
3. Pour the mixture into heavy bottomed pan and cook the mixture in a medium heat.
4. Keep stirring until the mixture gets thick and leaves the sides of the pan.
5. Let it cool for 10 minutes.
6. Now add the rest of the milk powder slowly at a time and mix well.
7. Don't mix all at once; it will make the mixture dry. The mixture should be soft and pliable to make pedas.
8. Use the round cutter to cut the pedas or use your hand to shape into round balls.
9. You can decorate the peda with chopped pistachios.

Rava Ladoo (Semolina Laddu)

Serves: 2-4

Ingredients:

- 500 g semolina (roasted)
- 200 g sugar
- 150 ml condensed milk
- 200 g grated coconut (lightly roasted)
- 50 g cashew nuts
- 50 g raisins/sultanas
- 4 tablespoons water
- 3 tablespoons ghee
- 1 teaspoon cardamom powder

Method:

1. Heat the ghee in a pan, when it is hot enough, add the cashew nuts and fry until slightly brown.
2. Add the raisins and when it is balloon up remove from heat and set aside.
3. Add grated fresh coconut and roast until golden brown.
4. In a same pan add semolina roast until the aroma starts to coming out.
5. Meanwhile boil the sugar and water. When it reaches the sticky consistency, remove from heat and set aside.
6. Take a big bowl and add the roasted rava, roasted coconut, cardamom powder, cashew nuts and raisins.
7. Pour the condensed milk over the mixture and mix everything until well combined.
8. Apply little ghee on your palm.
9. Add a few teaspoons of the sugar syrup and mix it with rava mixture and mold it into the size of a ball. Make sure

the syrup is little warm when you roll the ladoos into balls.
10. Repeat the same process for the remaining ladoos.
11. Rava ladoos can keep well in room temperature for up to 2-3 days.
12. Please refrigerate any leftover and finish it within one week.
13. Enjoy!

Condensed Milk Ice Cream

Serves: 1-2

Ingredients:

- 600 ml thickened cream
- 250 ml condensed milk
- 2 teaspoons vanilla extract

Method:

1. Using an electric mixer beat the cream until thick and creamy.
2. Add the condensed milk and vanilla, beat for another five minutes until thick and creamy.
3. Pour mixture into prepared pan; cover with plastic wrap and freeze for 6 hours or until frozen.

Family Chocolate Cake

Serves: 4-6

Ingredients:

- 230 g self-rising flour
- 125 g butter
- 330 g caster sugar
- 2 medium-large eggs (lightly beaten)
- 20 g cocoa powder
- 1 cup water
- ½ teaspoon bicarbonate of soda

For fudge frosting:

- 50 g caster sugar
- 120 g icing sugar
- 45 g butter
- 20 g cocoa powder
- 40 ml water

Method:

1. Preheat the oven to 180°c.
2. Line the cake tin with baking paper or grease proof paper, then brush the paper evenly with little butter.
3. Sift the cocoa powder and bicarbonate of soda.
4. Combine the water, sugar, butter and sifted cocoa and soda in a medium sauce pan.
5. Stir over heat without boiling.
6. Wait until the sugar to dissolve.
7. Bring to a boil and then reduce the heat.
8. Simmer for 5 minutes.
9. Cool the mixture to room temperature.

10. Sift the self-rising flour and add the lightly beaten egg to a bowl.
11. Beat the Flour and egg for 1 minute and add the cooled chocolate mixture slowly at a time and beat until mixture is smooth and changed to paler color.
12. Pour the mixture into prepared baking tin.
13. Bake cake about 40-45 minutes.
14. To check whether the cake is done or not, insert a fine skewer into the center if it is come out clean without any moisture it is done.
15. Stand cake in dish 5 minutes before turning onto wire rack.
16. Turn the cake top side up to cool.

Preparing the fudge frosting:

1. Sift the cocoa and icing sugar.
2. Combine the butter, water and caster sugar in small sauce pan.
3. Stir over heat without boiling, until sugar dissolves.
4. Gradually stir the sifted icing sugar and cocoa mixture in hot butter mixture.
5. Cover and refrigerate for 25 minutes or until the frosting thickens.
6. Beat with wooden spoon until spreadable.
7. Serve this chocolate cake as dessert or as a tea time treat.
8. This cake will keep an airtight container or up to 3 days.

Aluwa

Serves: 4-5

Ingredients:

- 1 x 410 g (14 1/2 oz) cups sweetened condensed milk
- 125 g (4 oz) butter
- 2 tablespoons rose water
- 1 ½ cups sugar
- 1 ½ cups milk
- 1 cup cooked mashed potato
- 1 cup finely chopped cashew nuts (optional)
- 1 teaspoon ground cardamom (optional)

Method:

1. Put sugar, milk, condensed milk and ghee into a large heated saucepan (a nonstick pan is excellent for this).
2. Cook over medium heat, stirring constantly, until mixture reaches soft ball stage or 116°C (240°F) on a candy thermometer. (To test for softball stage, drop a little into a cup of ice-cold water.
3. If it firm enough to be molded into a soft ball. It has reached the required temperature. Remove from heat, add smoothly mashed potato and beat with a rotary beater until all lumps are beaten out.
4. If using a pan with nonstick lining, pour mixture into a bowl before doing this or the metal beaters will scratch the nonstick surface.
5. Return to heat and cook to soft ball stage or 116°C (240°F) once more.
6. Remove from heat, stir in nuts, rose water and cardamom and mix well.

7. Pour into a well buttered shallow dish or baking tin.
8. Pres lightly with a piece of buttered banana leaf or aluminum foil to smooth and flatten the surface.
9. Allow to cool and set, then cut into diamond shapes.

Avocado Crazy

Serves: 4-6

Ingredients:

- 3 large fully ripe avocados
- 1 cup cream
- caster sugar to taste
- dash of rum (optional)

Method:

1. Cut avocados in halves lengthways, remove seeds and reserve.
2. Scoop pulp from shells and mash smoothly with a fork.
3. Add sugar to taste and stir in the cream.
4. Put into serving bowl, return seeds to the pulp, cover closely with plastic wrap and chill before serving.
5. The presence of the seeds in the puree is said to keep the avocado from discoloring, but make sure that the surface is protected from air by putting the plastic on the surface of the mixture.
6. If you like, extra whipped and sweetened cream can be piped over the top of the dessert and a few paper-thin slices of avocado (sliced at the last moment and sprinkled with lemon juice) used for decoration.

Note:

- While some favor rum for flavoring, I prefer to let the delicate avocado flavor stand alone.

Bibikkan (Sri Lankan Coconut Cake)

Serves: 4-6

Ingredients:

- 1 lb. semolina
- ¼ lb. raisins
- 4 cups honey
- ¼ lb. flour
- 25 cashew nuts
- 2 cups scraped coconut
- 2 oz. butter
- rind of lime
- ¼ lb. sugar
- 2 teaspoons vanilla
- 1 teaspoon rose water
- ½ teaspoon cardamom
- ½ teaspoon cinnamon
- your preferred fruit (dates, ginger preserves, sultanas, chow-chow, etc.)

Method:

1. Add sugar and honey to scraped coconut and cook over slow flame until coconut is cooked.
2. Add all fruits and cool overnight.
3. Next day add butter semolina and flour to mixture.
4. Then add vanilla, rose water, cinnamon and cardamoms.
5. Bake in moderate heat.
6. Server and enjoy.

Sri Lankan Watalappan (Cardamom Spiced Coconut Custard)

Serves: 6

Ingredients:

- 4 medium-large whole eggs
- 2 egg yolks
- ½ lb. natural dark brown molasses sugar or finely grated kitul jaggery
- ⅛ cup hot water
- 3-4 cardamom pod seeds crushed (just over ¼ teaspoon)
- ¼ teaspoon of nutmeg (if using fresh nutmeg, use less as it will be more potent)
- 2 cups of thick coconut milk (first press milk). If the coconut milk is lumpy - which can happen in cold weather - warm it up to dissolve the lumps
- pinch of salt

Method:

1. Preheat oven to 320°F / 160°C
2. Oil and prepare 7-8, ½ cup capacity ramekins.
3. In a large bowl, combine the sugar and water and stir until it becomes a paste with no lumps (the sugar does not need to dissolve completely)
4. Add the eggs and egg yolk, spices and salt and whisk until well combined - i.e. till the egg mixture becomes very slightly thick (not the "ribbony stage", just enough to thoroughly mix the sugar and eggs). Take care not to make the egg mixture frothy.
5. Add the 2 cups of coconut milk and whisk well.

6. Pour the mix into the prepared ramekins (or a large dish if you prefer). Cover the ramekins / dish with foil.
7. Bake the ramekins/dish in a water bath for about 30 - 40 minutes for the ramekins and up to an hour if in a large dish, depending on the depth of it. You want the custard to set, but the middle to be very slightly wobbly.
8. Remove from the oven and let them cool for about 15 minutes in the water bath.
9. When cool enough to handle, remove them from the water bath and cover the ramekins with plastic wrap, and place it in the fridge to chill for at least 3 hours (longer for larger dishes). Best chilled overnight.
10. Serve as is, or with some cashew nuts on top.

Note:

You can also some add raisins and cashew nuts into the custard if you prefer.

Mung Kavum

Serves: 2-4

Ingredients:

- 1 lb. rice flour
- 2 lb. mung flour
- 3 cups coconut or kithul treacle (available in Sri Lankan grocery stores)
- 1 tablespoon ghee or butter
- 1 teaspoon salt
- vegetable oil for deep frying

Batter:

- ½ lb. rice flour
- 1 medium-large egg
- 1 cup coconut milk
- ½ teaspoon salt
- pinch of turmeric

Method:

1. Mix the rice and mung flour to get an even mixture.
2. Boil the treacle in a saucepan. Add the flour mix.
3. When the mixture starts to thicken add butter and salt.
4. Transfer the thickened mixture into an aluminum tray (cookie tray) and allow cooling. Add about 1/2 cup water into the saucepan, leave on the hot plate and stir until thick syrup like consistency. Remove from heat.
5. Add small amounts of this syrup to the flour mix in the aluminum tray and spread into 1/2 -1/4" thick block.
6. Cut into shapes. Prepare the batter by mixing the ingredients well.

7. Dip the above pieces in the batter and deep fry in vegetable oil.

Love Cake

Serves: 2-4

Ingredients:

- 750 g cashew nuts
- 12 medium-large eggs
- 1 lb. sugar
- 6 oz. pumpkin preserve
- 2 sheets oil paper
- ½ lb. semolina (wheatlets)
- ½ lb. butter
- ½ bottle Rose Essence
- ½ bottle Almond Essence
- ½ vine glass Brandy
- ½ vine glass Bees Honey

Batter:

- ½ teaspoon each of cardamom, cloves, cinnamon (in fine powder form)
- ½ teaspoon grated nutmeg
- ¾ teaspoon grated lime rind

Method:

1. Warm Semolina with a few lime leaves. Add the butter to it and heat until well mixed.
2. Keep overnight.
3. Beat egg yolks with sugar until nice and creamy with air bubbles forming.
4. Remove lime leaves from semolina. Add semolina and butter mixture to the egg and sugar mixture and beat well.

5. Add cashew nuts (cut) and mix well. Next add pumpkin preserve (cut).
6. Add Spices and essences and lime rind.
7. Beat 8 egg whites until nice and fluffy and gradually add to cake mixture. Do not make it too watery.
8. Line tray with newspaper, final layer buttered oil paper
9. Bake in slow oven.

Sri Lankan Christmas Cake

Serves: 8-12

Ingredients:

- 400g (14 oz) soft brown sugar
- 300g (10oz) sultanas
- 225g (8oz) candied ash pumpkin or crystallized pineapple
- 225g (8oz) cashew nuts chopped
- 225g (8oz) semolina
- 225g (8 oz) butter at room temperature
- 125g (4oz) currants
- 100g (3.5oz) chow (without syrup)
- 100g (3.5oz) stem ginger (without syrup)
- 100g (3.5oz) raisins
- 100g (3.5oz) glace cherries
- 50g (2oz) almonds chopped
- 50g (2 oz) candied peel
- 3 tablespoonful brandy
- 3 tablespoonsful rose water triple strength
- 2 tablespoonful honey
- 2 teaspoonful ground cinnamon
- 1 teaspoonful ground cardamom
- 1 tablespoonful vanilla
- 1/2 a nutmeg grated
- 1/2 teaspoonful ground cloves
- 12 size 2 eggs

Method:

1. Finely chop the fruit and the nuts. Put into a bowl together with the honey and essences (the brandy, rose water, vanilla) and the spices (nutmeg, cinnamon, cardamom and cloves). Mix thoroughly and leave covered for 24 hours.
2. Double line 2 cake tins of diameter 20 cm (8") with lightly- oiled greaseproof paper. Put the oven on to 140oC (275oF)
3. In a medium-sized bowl, mix together the semolina and the butter. Separate the eggs. In a large bowl, beat the egg yolks together with the sugar until pale. Mix in the semolina. Add the fruit, a little at a time using a cutting motion, to make sure that the cake batter is thoroughly mixed in with the dried fruit. This movement provides a lot of wrist exercise!
4. Whisk half the egg whites until stiff. (The rest can be used for meringues.) Add 4 tablespoonfuls of the egg whites and beat into cake mixture to slacken it. Fold the rest of the beaten egg whites and mix thoroughly. Put the cake mixture into the two tins and cook for about 1½ hours, or until a skewer when inserted comes out clean. Cool the cake on a wire rack. Once cold prick the surfaces with a skewer and pour two tablespoonfuls of brandy over each cake. Cover with foil, place in an airtight tin and leave for a week before icing.
5. Triple strength rosewater is available from chemist's shops. In Sri Lanka the Christmas cake is cut into pieces and individually wrapped and served during the festive season. The marzipan is made from ground cashew-nuts.

Conclusion

I want to thank you once again for purchasing this book.

Sri Lankan cuisine can be hot or very mild or can be combination being very much a question of individual preference. Sri Lankan food is unique for their Culture. Many Sinhala food items are derived from Chena cultivation. Sri Lankan cuisine plays a vital role in the islanders' life from the most auspicious Sinhala/ Hindu New Year to normal day-to-day practices. They make milk rice and special sweets with coconut milk, floor and Honey at cultural festivals. It is recognized as one of the sixty- four types of art, "Siu Seta kalawa". The curries come in many verities of colors and flavors blended in Sri Lankan Hot Spices has a great ayurvedic value when used in curries.

Most of the Sri Lankans eat vegetables. With a large community of farmers, the Rice and curry is the main food in Sri Lanka. Sri Lanka curries are known for their fiery hot spicy flavors and coconut milk is very distinct feature of Sri Lankan cuisine that different regions of country specialize in different types of dishes. The specialty in Sri Lankan food is that same food is differently made in different regions. Dishes from the North region of Sri Lanka have distinct south Indian flavors.

Just always remember that great food starts with great ingredients. Do not be afraid to season your dish and always taste as you cook to balance out the flavors. Cooking is a learning process, and you become a better cook each time you remake the dish that you want to master. This book will help you achieve that.

Thank you and all the best.

Other Books by Grizzly Publishing

"Jamaican Cookbook: Traditional Jamaican Recipes Made Easy"

https://www.amazon.com/dp/B07B68KL8D

"Brazilian Instant Pot Cookbook: Delicious Pressure Cooked Meals Made Fast and Easy"

https://www.amazon.com/dp/B078XBYP89

"Norwegian Cookbook: Traditional Scandinavian Recipes Made Easy"

https://www.amazon.com/dp/B079M2W223

"Casserole Cookbook: Delicious Casserole Recipes From Around The World"

https://www.amazon.com/dp/B07B6GV61Q

CPSIA information can be obtained
at www.ICGtesting.com
Printed in the USA
FSHW021218020119
54783FS